Saint Edward the Martyr

The Life, Recorded Miracles and
Supplicatory Canon

The Fathers of
Saint Edward Brotherhood

CONTENTS

ACKNOWLEDGEMENTS

This book is foremost a spiritual work for the edification of the faithful; our thanks to Metropolitan Ambrose of Methoni for blessing its publication. The Historical Notes chapter would not have been possible without the assistance of real historians, which we are not. We would like to thank Prof. Levi Roach of the University of Exeter for taking the time to answer our queries and for sending us source material. Prof. David Dumville has kindly allowed us to include his translation of a tenth century poem on Saint Edward. Our thanks to Prof. Claire Downham of the University of Liverpool and Dr. Sandra Hynes of Aberdeen University Press for their assistance in obtaining copyright permissions. We are grateful to Annie Price and Anna Harding of the University of Exeter Special Collections Archives for helping us access the Courtenay Arthur Ralegh Radford Collection and supplying us with digital images; the photograph of the site of Shaftesbury Abbey is from the collection of John M. Clarke. Thanks, as always, to Jon Davies of Knaphill Print for his advice. Finally, we would like to thank Anthony Bell for checking the manuscript references and for proof-reading; any errors that remain are our responsibility.

PREFACE

The earliest surviving Life of Saint Edward the Martyr, the *Passio Sancti Eadwardi*, is attributed to the eleventh century hagiographer Goscelin of Saint-Bertin. Goscelin claims to be rewriting an existing life and it is likely that his source is an early eleventh century life from Shaftesbury Abbey.

The Latin text of the *Passio* was published in Christine Fell's *Edward King and Martyr*, but this scholarly edition does not include an English translation.[1] Ryan Grant's *The Passion of St. Edward, King and Martyr* is the only readily available and accurate translation of Goscelin's *Passio*.[2]

The Life of Saint Edward included here is for the edification of Orthodox Christians and is not a literal translation of the Latin. Footnotes and explanations have been avoided within the Life itself; a discussion of historical issues follows in a separate chapter.

The spelling of Anglo-Saxon Christian names has been conformed to that used in Sir Frank Stenton's *Anglo-Saxon England*.[3] Ælfthryth is therefore preferred to Elfreda and Æthelred to Ethelred. For Anglo-Saxon names in common usage, however, the modern form is used (eg. Edward not Eadweard).

This volume also includes a revised edition of *The Recorded Miracles of Saint Edward the Martyr* which was first published in pamphlet form in 1984 by King Edward Orthodox Trust. The author, John Wilson-Claridge, was the finder and donor of the relics to the Orthodox Church. Although his family name was Claridge, he preferred the hyphenated form 'Wilson-Claridge' in latter years.

---

1 C. Fell, *Edward King and Martyr* (Leeds: University of Leeds School of English, 1971)

[2] R. Grant (trans.), *The Passion of St. Edward, King and Martyr* (Cincinnati: Saragossa Press, 2020)

3 F. Stenton, *Anglo-Saxon England* (Oxford: Oxford University Press, 1971)

Among Angles has there not a worse deed been done than this
since they first sought out Britain's land.
Men murdered him, but God glorified him.
He was in life an earthly king;
He is now, after death, a heavenly saint.
Him would not his earthly kinsmen avenge,
But him hath his heavenly Father greatly avenged.
Earthly murderers would fain blot out his memory on earth,
But the lofty Avenger hath spread abroad
His memory in the heavens and on the earth.
They who would not earlier to his living body bow down,
These now humbly on knees bend to his dead bones.
Now we perceive that men's wisdom
And their devices and their counsels
Are all worthless against God's purpose.

Anglo-Saxon Chronicle

INTRODUCTION

The reign of Saint Edward as King of England (975-978) was brief, being cut short by his martyrdom. At this time, the eastern and western parts of the Church were united and shared the same Orthodox faith. However, the Church of Rome's decision to change the Christian Creed led eventually to a final separation in 1054 known as the Great Schism.

The Orthodox Church recognises the pre-schism western saints but their lives are not as familiar to the Orthodox faithful as those of the saints of the east. In Orthodoxy, Saint Edward the Martyr is also commemorated as a Passion-bearer. This title is given to rulers who were martyred for their defence of Orthodox principles. The Princes Boris and Gleb (24 July) and the Russian Royal Martyrs (4 July) are also Passion-bearers.

By the mid-tenth century the monastic life of the English Church was in a parlous state. King Edgar the Peaceable, Saint Edward's father, initiated a much needed revival, expanding the monastic estates at the expense of powerful land-owning magnates. Saint Edward continued this revival, and his support of traditional monasticism led eventually to his murder.

Saint Edward quickly found a place in the Anglo-Saxon calendar of saints; his shrine at Shaftesbury attracted pilgrims from all over the country and portions of his relics were distributed to abbeys in both England and continental Europe. The shrine was destroyed in the dissolution of the monasteries under Henry VIII; the relics disappeared and were presumed lost until their discovery in 1931 by John Wilson-Claridge.

It was Wilson-Claridge's desire that Saint Edward's relics should be available for veneration by the Christian faithful. After a long period of negotiations, and a lengthy court case, the relics were enshrined on 16 September 1984 at the Shrine Church in Brookwood, Surrey, where they remain today in the custody of Saint Edward Brotherhood.

The Shrine of Saint Edward the Martyr

THE LIFE OF SAINT EDWARD THE MARTYR

The renowned King Edward was descended from an exalted and noble line of ancient kings. He was baptised by the holy hierarch Dunstan the Archbishop of Canterbury and through his uprightness of life he surpassed in virtue all those rulers who had preceded him.

Edward's father, King Edgar, although mindful of the things of God, increased his earthly kingdom and subjected under his rule the kings of the regions of Britain. In answer to the petitions of Archbishop Dunstan and Bishop Æthelwold of Winchester, King Edgar began to restore the many deserted or neglected monasteries at his own expense. He supported the construction of new monasteries and convents and ordered that the abbots and monks abiding in them were to live under strict discipline. In other places, he established communities of nuns.

King Edgar, in his desire to put the affairs of the Church into good order, supported the inner life of the Church as well as the outward. He decreed that, as a beneficent pastor, he would care for the monks by visiting them frequently and encouraging them. His wife, also, looked after the convents as a most pious mother. This was done to preserve decorum, with a man caring for the monks and a woman, the nuns.

The aforesaid Edward was of good character, and his mind in no way wandered in lascivious thoughts, nor did he surrender himself to the enticing carnal passions. On the contrary, he was zealous to please God by uprightness of body and soul, and to be regarded by all with affection. Edgar, seeing his son cultivating such a noble character, rejoiced over his wisdom and diligence in good works.

King Edgar had another son named Æthelred from a later marriage to Ælfthryth, but he decreed that, following the hereditary custom, his eldest son Edward should succeed to the throne upon his death.

After expanding and uniting his kingdom and presiding over a period of peace and tranquillity, Edgar was taken from this life to eternal rest in the year of the Lord 975 in the sixteenth year of his rule on the eighth day of July.

After Edgar's death, his eldest son Edward, by the will of his father, was chosen to govern the realm by Saint Dunstan and many of the magnates, but certain others objected. These men interrupted Edward's coronation to voice their objections, but Saint Dunstan, taking hold of his staff and placing it in the midst of all, carried on the service with the rest of the bishops. The Archbishop crowned Edward having cared for him as a father from childhood and having loved him with paternal affection.

When Saint Edward was elevated to the throne of the kingdom, he was guided by the Lord, the King of Kings, in the ways of justice and truth and by God's help his days increased. He trusted in God with a pure disposition of soul and profound humility.

Edward increased in virtue even whilst honoured as king. He avoided youthful impulses and rash decisions, relying instead on the counsels and advice of Saint Dunstan. He exercised wise judgment in all things, not only considering matters carefully, but also relying on the advice of learned religious men and magnates of the land.

Following the custom of his father, he was not afraid to deal harshly and swiftly with heathen invaders and transgressors. He displayed his military prowess and courage in equal measure with his wise governance of matters concerning the Church. Pious lay people and monastics, however, he protected from every turmoil and threat of violence with care, following the custom of his father.

Edward also carried out a daily duty of feeding the hungry, setting aright the poor and clothing the naked, reckoning the time spent in such things to be of great profit. The English people experienced an abiding peace and great prosperity and were filled with joy on seeing their king pursuing such policies while still in the flower of youth. He was good-natured in all things, praiseworthy in almsgiving, comely and joyful in face, acclaimed in counsel and wisdom.

But the enemy of every good, the devil, who hates those who are content, desiring to disturb the peace of the English realm, tempted Edward's step-mother, Ælfthryth, who became filled with hatred for the new king. Her arrogant cunning, which is so abhorrent, particularly in a woman, is apparent from the way in which events came to pass.

After the fire of hatred was lit within her soul, she began to consider ways in which the young king could be removed and replaced by her own son, Æthelred. To do this, she needed the help of some of the most powerful magnates of the realm, so the new king could be installed without opposition from the people.

She, after turning things over in her mind for a while, approached certain magnates and opened her heart to them, pleading with them to come together and agree to her plans. Thus, they began to plot together. The treacherous magnates agreed to conspire with her to murder the king, and put their plans into action without delay.

At this time, King Edward had held the hereditary sceptre of the kingdom for three and a half years. One day he went hunting with some companions near a village called Wareham. The surrounding area was open ground, but now it is overgrown with trees and thin brush.

Remembering that his young half-brother lived nearby, Edward decided to call upon him, because he loved Æthelred with a pure and honest heart. Æthelred had been raised by his mother in a house near the place called Corfe by its inhabitants and where there now stands a famous fortress.

Edward had ridden hard in pursuit of his quarry and had left his retinue far behind. Seeing the house at the distance of a mere spear's throw, he approached it as an innocent lamb without fear or suspicions; his conscience being clear, he feared no retribution from any that he had offended.

As they saw the king approaching, Ælfthryth's attendants informed this most impious queen that the king was nearby. She, giving into wicked passions and embracing treachery to fulfil her wicked desires, rejoiced in heart that the time had come.

She and her attendants went forth, outwardly rejoicing at the king's arrival, but inwardly their hearts were full of iniquity. They greeted Edward with friendliness and invited him to be their guest. He declined their offer, and asked to see his brother.

Ælfthryth then ordered a drink to be brought to distract the king so that perhaps a moment might present itself to carry out her plan. One of her retinue, filled with bestial wickedness, feigning goodwill and imitating Judas the betrayer of the Saviour, offered his king the kiss of peace in order to dispel any suspicion that Edward might have.

Edward took the drink from the cup-bearer, but before he had the chance to quench his thirst, the servant that had given him the kiss launched himself at the king from behind and pierced his vitals with a dagger. Being stricken with a mortal wound, Edward twisted in his saddle as his horse, which bolted from fear, dragged Edward along with it.

So the beloved of God died, but he exchanged earthly things for the heavenly, and received a heavenly imperishable crown in exchange for the crown of an earthly perishable kingdom. This took place in the 978th year of the Incarnate Word and, although it is impious to record, during the Great Fast, on the 18th day of March.

All this was ordained by Divine Providence so that he who had wearied his body by fasting and good works according to the Christian tradition, thus preparing himself for the day of the Lord's resurrection, might be crowned with a good end. In the midst of good works, he was taken into the embrace of Christ in the heavens, because, as the Judge of all has decreed, everyone will be judged in the state in which he is found.

Queen Ælfthryth hearing that Edward had fallen from his horse, not satiated by her outpouring of wickedness ordered his body to be hidden as soon as possible, and it was thrown into a small hut – lest the crime should become widely known. Those under her command dragged the body away by the feet and covered it with straw.

The hut in which the body was concealed was the lowly home of a blind woman whom the queen supported by almsgiving. On the night following the murder, the blind woman saw the appearance of the glory of the Lord in her home where the body of the martyred king lay. The small hut was filled with an immeasurable splendour.

The poor woman, stricken with terror, prayed to the Almighty God for mercy and was granted to receive her sight by the workings of divine grace. The Christian faithful later erected a small church in this place as a witness of the miracle.

As dawn broke, Ælfthryth learned that the blind woman had received the gift of sight. The queen was troubled in mind, fearing that her abhorrent deed would come to light if she did not hide the body of the martyr more securely. She ordered that it be hidden in a unpopulated marshy area to prevent further discovery.

After this was done, an edict was proclaimed that no one should weep over Edward's demise or even speak of it. By doing this, the queen desired to blot out his memory from the earth. Ælfthryth then fled to a large house in Bere Regis which she owned, thereby distancing herself from the scene so that no one would suspect her involvement.

Meanwhile her young son Æthelred was inconsolable with grief over the cruel murder of his brother Edward. So much so, that he could not control his mourning or his tears. His grief enraged his mother so much that she violently beat him with a bunch of candles that she had near at hand until he stopped his weeping. It is said that, from this time forth, Æthelred so hated candles that he forbade them to be lighted in his presence.

After some time the relics of the martyr Edward were made known to the world when a pillar of fire appeared above the place in which they lay. Pious men from Wareham, seeing this light, gathered the relics and carried them to a nearby house.

A large crowd gathered, and with weeping cried out: 'What comfort can we hope for now after these things? Who will free us from the attacks of enemies now that our shepherd has been struck down? Our joys have perished; the unity of our nation and the treaties of peace have become of none effect.'

With the voices of mourning, the venerable relics were brought to the church of the Mother of God in Wareham and were laid to rest on the 13th day of February. A wooden church built at this place by the monks is still there in our time. At the place where the saint's body had first lain, a fountain of healing water sprang forth which is even now called the Spring of Saint Edward. Many healings are granted at this spring to the praise of our Lord Jesus Christ.

By this time the news of King Edward's murder had spread throughout the English land and the treachery of the queen was exposed. The veneration of the innocent king spread and the holiness of his life was preached everywhere.

A certain magnate named Ælfhere was filled with immense joy on hearing that the relics had been miraculously discovered. Desiring to show obedience to his king as to one living, he proposed that they should be translated to a more worthy place.

He invited bishops, abbots and many nobles of the kingdom and asked them to support his endeavours. He also sent a message to the Abbess Wulfthryth of Wilton to ask her community to perform the appropriate funeral rites. This monastery was the place of repentance of Edith, the daughter of King Edgar, renowned for the uprightness of her life and piety.

Bishops and abbots having gathered together, Ælfhere and a multitude of the faithful arrived at Wareham where the body of the man of God lay. In the sight of all the people, the body was removed from the earth incorrupt. The bishops and the magnates with hymns and praises glorified God who had deigned to reveal the innocence of his martyr with such a sign.

Edward's sister Edith, running forward, embraced the body and whilst holding those cherished hands, bestowed many kisses upon them. She watered his face with her tears, but she gained no comfort from her sighs, or spiritual joy from the glorification of her brother by God.

The relics were taken up and placed on a bier with great solemnity and were translated to the monastery at Shaftesbury dedicated to the Mother of God.

Multitudes of lay people, hearing of the miracles that had occurred, flocked to the convent. Two poor men, paralysed with an illness so severe that they could barely walk except on their hands and knees, arrived with the multitude and beseeched God and Saint Edward to heal them of their disease. When they approached the relics, they were restored to full health. On seeing this miracle, the people rejoiced and all glorified God in His saint.

Queen Ælfthryth on hearing of the miracles wrought by the saint, repented of her wicked deeds. Mounting her horse she made haste to ask forgiveness for her crime. However, she was prevented by a hidden force, for when she mounted to ride with her retinue her horse refused to move. Trying to turn the horse this way and that using the bridle she could not make the horse move either with threats or kicks and she realised that she was held back by her sins.

Dismounting the horse, she prepared to proceed on foot, and demonstrating her full repentance she made it known that all these things had come to pass because of the crime that she had committed against the man of God.

The venerable body was laid to rest at the convent, and was buried in the north part of the altar on the 18th day of February. Many healings were granted to the sick through the intercessions of the saint.

Among those healed was a certain married woman, living in one of the remotest parts of England who had been overcome with weakness. Prayers were said for her by the monastics, and on a certain night Saint Edward appeared to her in a vision and said: 'When thou arisest in the morning, go at once to the place where I am buried and thou shalt receive a new and necessary shoe for your weakness.' It can be surmised, therefore, that this woman was suffering from severe lameness and through the phrase 'new shoe' the healing of her feet was indicated.

On waking, she related the dream to a neighbour since she distrusted it, thinking it was a delusion. When, however, she failed to obey the saint, he appeared again to her in a vision and said: 'Why dost thou spurn my commands and thereby neglect thy healing? Go to my tomb and there thou wilt be released from thine infirmity.'

After coming to her senses, she said: 'Who art thou, O Lord, and where shall I find thy tomb?' He answered: 'I am King Edward, recently slain by unjust hands, and I am buried in the Church of the Mother of God in Shaftesbury.'

On waking, the woman pondering on what she had seen, took necessary provisions for the journey and set forth for the convent. On arriving there she entreated God and Saint Edward with a humble heart and was restored to health.

A great many miracles were granted at the tomb of the saint, but many of these have not been committed to writing due our negligence. After some time, through the Providence of God, the relics of the saint began to rise from the ground. Through this sign and other wonders it became clear that the saint wished to be transferred from this dwelling place.

Saint Edward also appeared to a certain man in a vision and said: 'Go to the renowned monastery in Shaftesbury and to the virgin Abbess Æthelfreda who is in charge there and give these commands. You will say, therefore, that I wish to be removed from this place in which I have lain for a long time and that she should tell my brother without delay to order this on my behalf.'

This man, rising early in the morning and considering the vision which he had been granted went swiftly to Abbess Æthelfreda as he had been commanded by the saint and told her of all the things which had been revealed to him. She, giving thanks to Almighty God, related to King Æthelred all that had occurred, including, with much devotion, the elevation of Saint Edward's tomb.

The king, being filled with immeasurable joy and gladness on hearing of the glorification of his brother, made known his desire to be present at the translation. However, pressed in from every side by invasions of the enemy he could scarcely be present. Instead, he ordered messengers to be sent to Bishop Wulfsige of Sherborne and Abbot Ælfsige of New Minster, Winchester, commanding that they should transfer the body of his brother to a more worthy place.

These venerable men, obeying the royal command, gathered at the monastery with a multitude of the faithful and opened the tomb with great reverence and spiritual rejoicing. Such a wonderful fragrance arose from the tomb that those present thought they had been translated to Paradise.

The bishops, approaching devoutly, took up the sacred relics from the tomb and placed them in a casket lovingly prepared. They interred them in the altar with the other relics of the saint in a rite of godly rejoicing. The relics of the saint were translated on the 20th day of June 1001.

HISTORICAL NOTES

The Monastic Reforms of King Edgar

Saint Edward's father, King Edgar the Peaceable, reigned from 959–975. In 973, towards the very end of his reign, he was the first man to be consecrated King of England during a service compiled by Saint Dunstan the Archbishop of Canterbury. Ælfric, the tenth century abbot of Eynsham, recalls Edgar's reign as follows:

> *Edgar, the noble and resolute king, mightiest of all the kings of the English people, spread the praise of God everywhere among his people; and God subdued his enemies for him always, and subjected themselves to him in respect of whatever he might wish; and he was praised far and wide throughout the realm.*[4]

Saint Dunstan worked closely with King Edgar to reinvigorate monastic life in England which was in a parlous state due to decades of spiritual neglect and the destruction of numerous monasteries and convents by the Vikings. On Saint Dunstan's return from exile in 957, Glastonbury and Abingdon were the only properly functioning monasteries in England.

The monarch's active involvement was crucial if any reinvigoration of monastic life was to be successful. In fact, during Edgar's reign approximately twenty-two monastic houses were established, and he personally directed that all monasteries, both new and existing, should follow the Rule of Saint Benedict.[5] King Edgar's Charter to Ely Abbey states:

> *I desire now with God's guidance to fill the deserted minsters everywhere in my dominion with monks and also with*

---

[4] D. N. Dumville, *Wessex and England from Alfred to Edgar* (Woodbridge: The Boydell Press 1992) p. 141

[5] C. Holdsworth, 'Benedictine monks and nuns of the 10th century' in L. Keen (ed.) *Studies in the History of Shaftesbury Abbey* (Dorchester: Dorchester County Council 1999) p. 73

nuns... and to renew the worship of God, which has been neglected. And the nuns shall live their life according to the rule of the holy Benedict.[6]

The Rule of Saint Benedict requires monastics to renounce their possessions and wealth. This traditional form of monasticism is called *cenobitic* in Orthodoxy which is derived from the Greek word *koinobion* meaning 'community life'.

Before Edgar's reign, donations of land to individual monks or nuns were commonplace, but his reforms outlawed this practice. Saint Æthelwold of Winchester's account of monasticism at this time shows that monastic regulation and reinvigoration was long overdue:

We also instruct abbesses to be deeply loyal and to serve the precepts of the holy rule with all their hearts, and to enjoin the commands of God Almighty, so that none of them shall presume senselessly to give God's estates either to kinsmen or secular grand persons neither for money nor for flattery.[7]

This reform movement, however, generated opposition from the magnates who had seen their estates shrink in size as monasteries acquired more property. Undoubtedly many had only agreed to sell or donate land under pressure from King Edgar.

The opinions of these magnates on monastic expansion were significant. Tenth century English kings ruled most of the territory now known as England, but the country was far from being unified and a monarch needed the support of the magnates in order to govern the country effectively.

---

[6] M. Deanesly, *The Pre-conquest Church in England* (London: Adam & Charles Black, 1963) p. 305

[7] B. Yorke, 'Sisters under the skin? Anglo-Saxon nuns and nunneries in southern England', *Reading Medieval Studies*, Vol. 15 (1989) pp. 106-7

The Motive for Saint Edward's Murder

On King Edgar's death, what historians call the 'anti-monastic reaction' gathered pace. This movement, however, was very different in character to the sixteenth century dissolution of the monasteries under Henry VIII.

This latter destruction of the monasteries was aimed at strengthening the position of Henry's new Church of England; as powerful centres of Roman Catholic faith and religious practice, the very existence of the monasteries posed a threat to the new Church. The dissolution began in 1536, and by 1540 monasteries were being closed at the rate of fifty a month. The closures were accompanied by the destruction or dismantling of shrines and the removal of images of the saints.

The leaders of the tenth century anti-monastic reaction, however, had no religious objection to the veneration of relics or monasticism. Ealdormen Ælfhere of Mercia and Æthelwine of East Anglia, the leading 'anti-monastics' of the period, were actually supporters of monasticism. Ælfhere was a patron of both Abingdon and Glastonbury Abbeys.

The motive for this reaction was financial and not religious. Magnates spared monasteries that they were connected to, but were prepared to seize land from others when it suited their interests. Their primary goal was to regain land and property. Professor Levi Roach explains as follows:

> There was, therefore, something of a reaction – or, perhaps more accurately: a series of local reactions – against reformed monastic houses at this point, whose power and influence had been a cause of jealousy amongst their lay neighbours. Many of these were new foundations (or refoundations) and the scale of their endowments must have caused major shifts in local land-holding patterns, shifts which cannot have been in the interests of all.[8]

---

[8] L. Roach, *Æthelred the Unready* (New Haven: Yale University Press, 2017) p. 67

The succession of a young king to the English throne must have provided considerable encouragement to discontented magnates; it would have allowed them to initiate actions which they would never have contemplated under King Edgar. However, it quickly became obvious that Edward would be continuing his father's support of the monasteries, guided by Archbishop Dunstan.

The anti-monastic faction evidently lacked coordination and clearly defined objectives. Nevertheless the threat to monasteries was real. The situation became so serious that Pope John XIV wrote to Ealdorman Ælfric warning him of excommunication if he failed to stop his aggression against Glastonbury Abbey. [9]

The *Passio* is unequivocal that Saint Edward's murder was orchestrated by Queen Ælfthryth and supported by certain magnates. The murder would thereby satisfy both parties; it would install Ælfthryth's son as king and also remove from the throne an important ally of the monastics.

The Succession Question

After the death of Saint Edward's mother Æthelflæd, Edgar married Wulfthryth with whom he had a daughter, Edith, who later entered the monastic life and is commemorated on 16 September. Edgar's third consort was Ælfthryth whom he married in 964 and who was anointed queen during the coronation of 973.

Ælfthryth bore Edgar two sons: Edmund, who died in infancy in 971 and Æthelred (*c*.966–1016) who later became King Æthelred the 'Unready' or 'Ill-counselled'. On the death of King Edgar in 975, Edward succeeded to the throne as Edgar's eldest son. The *Passio* records that objections were raised

---

[9] D. J. V. Fisher, 'The Anti-Monastic Reaction in the Reign of Edward the Martyr', *Cambridge Historical Journal*, Vol. 10, No. 3 (1952) p. 257

at Edward's coronation, but there is no hint of a succession dispute in the Anglo-Saxon Chronicle.[10]

The historian Eadmer (c.1060–c.1126) includes a letter in his personal manuscript from Prior Nicholas of Worcester which states that objectors were supporters of Æthelred.[11] Apparently they were of the opinion that because Æthelred's mother Ælfthryth had been consecrated queen whilst Edward's mother had not, Æthelred was the legitimate king.

However, the consecration in question is clearly the one in 973 which, according to Eadmer, Edgar had postponed of his own accord. As Æthelred was seven years old at this time, the consecration of his mother as queen does not benefit his claim at all.

The motive for Edgar's consecration towards the end of his reign has puzzled historians for decades. The service of 'sacring', or consecrating kings by anointing with oil, was already well established in Europe by 973, but there is no evidence of Edgar being consecrated prior to this date.

Earlier kings had been crowned when ascending the throne and Edgar is depicted wearing a crown in the frontispiece of the *New Minster Charter* whilst holding this document of 966.[12] However, only a previous consecration, not merely a coronation, can make sense of Eadmer's explanation.

A largely secular crowning ceremony is obviously not the consecration to which Eadmer is referring. Moreover, this consecration must have occurred sometime before 966 for

---

[10] The writing of the Anglo-Saxon Chronicle began during the reign of King Alfred the Great. The copies that have survived are referred to by their place of origin and by a letter: Winchester (A), Abingdon (B and C), Worcester (D), Peterborough (E) and Canterbury Bilingual Epitome (F). Other smaller fragments are in existence.

[11] W. Stubbs (ed.), *Memorials of Saint Dunstan, Archbishop of Canterbury* (London: Longman and Co., 1874) p. 423

[12] London, British Library, Cotton MS Vespasian A VIII fol. 2v.

Æthelred's supporters to claim that he was born from a consecrated queen.

It is evidently consecration, not coronation, that Edgar's contemporaries considered significant. The Winchester Chronicle (A), whilst only alluding to earlier coronations, celebrates Edgar's consecration as king in his thirtieth year on the Feast of Pentecost with a twenty line poem. Clearly, the poet did not believe that Edgar had previously been consecrated, although some historians propose that he had been, and possibly more than once.[13]

In addition, the Peterborough Chronicle (E) records that 'the *ætheling* Edgar was consecrated as king on the Feast of Pentecost on 11 May at the Hot Baths, in the 13th year after he succeeded to the kingdom; he was then 29 years old.'[14] The Anglo-Saxon word *ætheling* is equivalent to 'prince'. There seems no reason why the chronicler would have demoted a previously consecrated king.

The reason for the delay in consecration is unclear. One widely accepted theory is that Edgar waited until his thirtieth year, which is the minimum age for episcopal consecration. The choice of Pentecost for the ceremony supports this interpretation and there are many similarities between this regal consecration and the episcopal consecrations of the time.[15]

Another explanation for the delay is provided by the Anglo-Norman chronicler Gaimar who notes Saint Dunstan's displeasure at Edgar's relationship with Ælfthryth whilst his second wife, Wulfthryth, was still alive - albeit in a convent.[16] In putting

---

[13] For a discussion of these arguments see: E. John, 'King Edgar's Coronation' in *Orbis Britanniae and Other Studies* (Leicester: Leicester University Press, 1966) pp. 276- 289

[14] M. Swanton (trans, ed.) *The Anglo-Saxon Chronicles* (London: Phoenix Press, 2000) p. 119

[15] See A. Jones, 'The Significance of the Regal Consecration of Edgar in 973', *Journal of Ecclesiastical History*, Vol. 33, No. 3 (1982) pp. 375- 390

[16] B. Yorke, *Nunneries and the Anglo-Saxon Royal Houses* (London: Continuum, 2003) p. 168

away his wife, Edgar had violated the canons of the Church and Saint Dunstan was not afraid of speaking truth to power. It is possible that the Archbishop delayed the anointing until such time as Edgar had proved himself worthy of consecration.

Leaving the issue of consecration aside, there are indications that Æthelred could have been promoted as a legitimate successor to Edgar given that his elder brother Edmund (d.971) is given precedence over Edward in the witness list of the *New Minster Charter* of 966.[17]

The formulas and order of attestation in this charter are without precedent in Anglo-Saxon history. Ælfthryth attests before the bishops, with the sole exception of the Archbishop of Canterbury. Also, her status as the legitimate wife of Edgar is clearly stated, together with Edmund's legitimacy.

It is now accepted that the *New Minster Charter* was drafted by Saint Æthelwold of Winchester, an ally of Ælfthryth.[18] As such, it might represent a view of the succession not shared beyond the circle of Ælfthryth and her allied magnates. It is noteworthy that this charter contradicts a genealogy compiled during the brief period that King Edgar and all his sons were alive (*c.*966–*c.*971) which gives Edward precedence over both Edmund and Æthelred.[19]

There is no evidence, apart from Eadmer's twelfth century account, which is itself based on hearsay, 'that either Edward's or his mother's legitimacy was in question in 975'.[20] Indeed, Eadmer contradicts himself when he states in his *Life of Saint*

[17] London, British Library, Cotton MS Vespasian A VIII f. 30v.

[18] S. Miller, *Anglo-Saxon Charters IX: Charters of New Minster, Winchester* (London: British Academy, 2001) p. 108

[19] London, British Library, Cotton MS Tiberius B V fol. 23r. See D. N. Dumville, 'The Anglian collection of royal genealogies and lists', *Anglo-Saxon England* Vol. 5 (1977) p. 43

[20] A. Williams, *Æthelred the Unready the Ill-Counselled King* (London: Hambledon and London, 2003) p. 9

Dunstan that Edgar left the 'entire kingdom to his son Edward by hereditary right'.[21]

There is no evidence that the people regarded Edward as an unworthy successor to King Edgar – quite the opposite. The Peterborough Chronicle (E) entry for 979 pointedly records that Æthelred's accession was greeted with great rejoicing by the English magnates – it fails to mention any rejoicing among the people.

Dating the Martyrdom of Saint Edward

The question of whether Saint Edward was martyred in 978 or 979 has been the subject of some historical debate. The respected *Handbook of British Chronology* published by the Royal Historical Society records Saint Edward's death as occurring in 978.[22] There are, however, discrepancies in the Anglo-Saxon Chronicle.

The martyrdom of Saint Edward is dated 978 in the contemporary Winchester (A) and near-contemporary Abingdon (C) versions, but the later and closely related Worcester (D) and Peterborough (E) Chronicles date the martyrdom of Saint Edward and the accession of Æthelred to 979.[23]

Additional information can be gleaned from regnal tables (lists of kings in chronological order). Regnal tables in the New Minster *Liber Vitae* and *Textus Roffensis* assign Saint Edward a reign of three years eight months (presumably from July 975 to March 979).[24]

---

[21] A. J. Turner and B. J. Muir (eds.), *Eadmer of Canterbury: Lives and Miracles of Saints Oda, Dunstan, and Oswald* (Oxford Medieval Texts) (Oxford: Oxford University Press, 2006) p. 145

[22] D. N. Dumville, 'Kings of England (1) 927-1066' in E. B. Fryde, D. E. Greenway et al. (eds.) *Handbook of British Chronology* (London: Royal Historical Society, 1986) p. 27

[23] The *Passio* dates the martyrdom to 981 which is obviously an error.

[24] D. N. Dumville, 'The Death of King Edward the Martyr – 18 March 979?',

On the other hand, an eleventh century regnal table preserved in the British Library records that King Edward reigned for only three years.[25] This would place his martyrdom in 978, assuming that rounding up was used to calculate reign length.

In this particular table, the length of reign is denoted by Roman numerals, but Æthelred's reign length is replaced by a small design, added by the scribe to indicate a blank in the exemplar he was copying from. The exemplar can therefore be dated to the reign of Æthelred, the successor of Saint Edward. The early date of this table lends support to those who believe that the martyrdom occurred in 978.

Wilson-Claridge strongly advocates 979 in the *Recorded Miracles of Saint Edward the Martyr* and cites the *Glastonbury Easter Table* as settling the debate beyond doubt. This table, which forms part of the *Leofric Missal*, does indeed date the death of Saint Edward to 979.[26] However, King Edgar's death is entered under the year 976 (a year later than that in the Worcester Chronicle (D)). It is therefore reasonable to suppose that the date of Saint Edward's death might also be a year advanced.

Another Easter Table in the *Aelfwine Prayerbook* compiled at New Minster, Winchester, in the third decade of the eleventh century dates the martyrdom to 978.[27]

Additional evidence is provided by diplomas issued by King Æthelred. A royal diploma or charter is an official document making a grant of land or recording a privilege; diplomas were issued by the king in the presence of witnesses. Simon Keynes has identified four diplomas which indicate that

---

Anglo-Saxon, Vol.1 (2007) p. 275

[25] London, British Library, MS Cotton Tiberius B.V fol. 22r.

[26] Oxford, University of Oxford, Bodleian Library, MS. Bodl. 579 fol. 53r.

[27] London, British Library, MS Cotton Titus D XXVII fol. 14v..

Æthelred's reign started in 978 and six charters that show he began his reign in 979.[28]

According to Keynes, the only logical explanation for the dating of these diplomas is that some are dated from Æthelred's accession on 18 March 978 and the others from his consecration on 4 May 979.

David Dumville, in his contribution to the *Handbook of British Chronology*, dates the martyrdom to 978.[29] However, in more recent research, he has concluded that the contradictions in the charter evidence are a fatal flaw in the 978 argument.[30] He provides further evidence in the form of a contemporary poem included in the *Life of Saint Cuthbert* which says King Edward reigned for three and a half years, placing his martyrdom in 979. [31]

Dumville is the only eminent historian currently advocating 979. The chronology of this period is undoubtedly complicated, and while it is possible that the martyrdom occurred in 979, according to Levi Roach, this is an improbable alternative to 978.[32]

---

[28] S. Keynes, *The Diplomas of King Æthelred 'the Unready' 978–1016* (Cambridge: Cambridge University Press, 1980) p. 233

[29] Dumville, 'Kings of England (1) 927-1066' p. 27

[30] Dumville, 'The Death of King Edward the Martyr - 18 March 979?' p. 274

[31] London, British Library, MS Harley 1117 fol. 1r.

[32] Personal correspondence with the author.

The Translations of the Sacred Relics

The Peterborough (E) Chronicle records that Saint Edward was buried at Wareham without any royal honours, and that in the following year, Ealdorman Ælfhere of Mercia translated the relics to Shaftesbury with much honour. The *Vita Oswaldi* also refers to a translation to Shaftesbury in the year following Edward's murder:

> *The glorious Ealdorman Ælfhere came with a crowd of people and commanded that his body be raised from the ground; the body was found to be uncorrupt and was duly carried to the place where they gave him a worthy burial.*[33]

According to the *Passio*, however, following their miraculous discovery, the relics were first translated to the Church of the Mother of God at Wareham on 13 February. A translation of the relics on this date is recorded in five pre-1100 calendars.[34] The *Passio* also records the arrival of the relics at Shaftesbury on 18 February, but gives no indication of the year this occurred.

The mid-eleventh century missal, *The Red Book of Darley*, originating from Sherborne Abbey, Dorset includes two translations: 13 February and 18 February.[35] The mid-twelfth century *Winchester Psalter* has four entries for Saint Edward: 13 February for the translation, 18 February for the arrival (*adventus*) at Shaftesbury, 18 March for the martyrdom and 20 June for the elevation of the relics at Shaftesbury.[36]

---

[33] S. Ridyard, *The Royal Saints of Anglo-Saxon England* (Cambridge: Cambridge University Press, 1988) p. 155

[34] R. Rushworth, *Saints in English Kalendars before A.D. 1100* (London: Henry Bradshaw Society, 2008) Table II

[35] Cambridge, University of Cambridge, Corpus Christi College MS 422 p. 30

[36] London, British Library, MS Cotton Nero C IV fol. 42v. This Psalter is almost certainly a copy of a much earlier exemplar. Arundel MS 60, for example, was compiled during the same period, but Francis Wormald has demonstrated

There seems to be no doubt that the relics remained at Wareham for a time. The calendar evidence for a translation on 13 February is strong. The question remains whether this translation was to, or from, Wareham.

It is possible that, in the year following the martyrdom, a procession set out on 13 February from Wareham and arrived at Shaftesbury on 18 February – a feasible journey by foot even considering the short days at the time of year. It is also possible, as the *Passio* states, that the relics were translated on 13 February to Wareham, remained there a whole year, and were then translated to Shaftesbury.

It is significant that Saint Edward's relics were not taken to Winchester where earlier West Saxon kings had been buried, or to Glastonbury to join his father, King Edgar. Saint Edward's grandmother, Saint Ælfgifu, was already interred at the Abbey, but it was not a royal burial ground. Saint Edward remains the only Anglo-Saxon king ever to have been buried at Shaftesbury.

This separation of Saint Edward from his royal ancestors appears to strengthen the position of the new king. It is reasonable to suppose that it could have been instigated by Ælfthryth and her allies. However, it is more likely that the translation to Shaftesbury was a response to requests from the nuns of the convent to possess the relics of the saint.[37]

---

that it was copied practically without alteration from an exemplar composed in Winchester between 988 and 1012. See: F. Wormald, 'The English Saints in the Litany in Arundel MS. 60', *Analecta Bollandiana* Vol. 61, No. 1-2 (1946) pp. 72-86

[37] See N. Marafioti, *The King's Body: Burial and Succession in Late Anglo-Saxon England.* (Toronto: University of Toronto Press, 2014) p. 181

A Contemporary Poem

The following poem is written from the point of view of an eye-witness to the translation of the relics of Saint Edward from Wareham to Shaftesbury. The poet could plausibly have been a nun from the Abbey itself. The original twenty-six line Latin poem is included in a Life of Saint Cuthbert originating from Canterbury Cathedral towards the end of the tenth century.[38]

The nature of the *ordo* (order) which commissioned the poem is unknown, but it is significant that it is preserved in a Canterbury manuscript. The Canterbury Bilingual Epitome Chronicle (F) records that Archbishop Dunstan was present at the translation, but although this is highly likely, his presence is not corroborated by other sources.[39]

This translation is by Professor David Dumville and first appeared in the journal *Anglo-Saxon*.[40] It is reproduced here in full by kind permission of the translator.

All must remember the day on which Eadweard, the greatest king of the English was laid low, slain by a dreadful death. It is certain that he died through envy, at the hands of his own kin. He had ruled the English for three and a half years. Alas, they did not fear thus to deceive the hand of their master. For allied with those above, he has sought out Christ among the stars. After a short time he enjoys an honourable support, without doubt experiencing Christ's aid.

He is being lifted from the tomb in which he lay buried before and is being carried on a bier, worthily accompanied by his people. But beside him are the foremost nobles and many priests, among whom was Ælfhere, most worthy leader.

---

[38] London, British Library, MS Harley 1117 fol. 1r.
[39] Dumville, 'The death of King Edward the Martyr – 18 March 979?' p. 278
[40] *Ibid.*

Then they reach the city which is called Shaftesbury. There is groaning, and their hearts stir up long weeping. They conduct the burial rites and sing his praises. His body is returned to the ground and his spirit to Olympus. Carried on a successful journey by an angelic choir, now he enters heaven because he spattered the earth with his blood; by his murder in the flesh he has deserved to climb to heaven. O man most blessed in his leaving of the prison of the flesh! For in return for his death he has gained a most excellent reward.

Now that the poem has been completed which the *ordo* had requested to be made, we make an end of writing verse with the thumb. You, brother, I ask, though not in polished writing, may the acts of our agreement be secret in all ways. Please pour forth prayers for him in a most earnest request.

The Glorification of Saint Edward

Queen Ælfthryth, although she had succeeded in placing her son on the throne, retired from public life. She was tonsured a nun and died around 999 whilst presiding over the convent at Wherwell which, according to William of Malmesbury, she founded as an act of repentance for the murder of Saint Edward.

The veneration of Saint Edward spread quickly; his feast day is included in the *Leofric Missal* and the *Salisbury Psalter*, both compiled in the late tenth century. A royal diploma issued by King Æthelred in 1001 refers to '[God's] saint, my brother Edward, whom, drenched in his own blood, the Lord has seen fit to magnify in our time through many miracles'.[41] This diploma also placed the *coenobium* of Bradford-on-Avon under the authority of Shaftesbury Abbey in order for the former to become a hiding place for the relics of the martyr Edward in case of Danish invasion.

---

[41] Ridyard, *The Royal Saints of Anglo-Saxon England* p. 156

King Æthelred's support for his brother's sanctity led to the opening of his tomb and the enshrinement of his relics within the Abbey church on June 20 1001.

Furthermore, in 1008, a royal assembly convened at Enham in Hampshire under the guidance of Ælfheah Archbishop of Canterbury and Wulfstan Archbishop of York, decreed that the feast of Saint Edward 'is to be celebrated over all England on 18 March'.[42] Some have argued that this instruction is a later addition to the record of the proceedings, but Simon Keynes has concluded that the text is authoritative.[43]

There is no doubt that Saint Edward's veneration was widespread by the early eleventh century. The martyrdom of Saint Edward is dated 18 March in seventeen pre-1100 calendars, and in eight of them the entry is written in capitals letters signifying an important festival.[44]

The Abbey itself underwent many architectural changes and additions over the centuries. In the late eleventh century church, Saint Edward's shrine was situated on the north side of the chancel; the empty tomb, lined with finely dressed stone, was discovered in 1861. In the fourteenth century, the relics were translated to a new chapel with a crypt beneath it. [45]

The relics of Saint Edward were venerated in the Abbey shrine until the dissolution of the monasteries in the reign of King Henry VIII. On 23 March 1539, Shaftesbury Abbey was surrendered to the King's Commissioner, Sir John Tregonwell. By the middle of the same century the abbey was in ruins.

---

[42] London, British Library, MS Cotton Nero A i fol. 91r.

[43] S. Keynes, 'An Abbot, and Archbishop, and the Viking raids 1006-7 and 1009-10', *Anglo-Saxon England*, Vol. 36 (2007) p. 178

[44] Rushworth, *Saints in English Kalendars before A.D. 1100*, Table III

[45] Royal Commission on Historical Monuments, *An inventory of Historical Monuments in the County of Dorset*, Vol. 4 North Dorset (London: HMSO, 1972) p. 58

The Discovery of the Relics

The historical evidence that the relics were once enshrined at Shaftesbury is overwhelming.[46] The relics survived the destruction of both the shrine and the Abbey. They remained concealed in a hastily constructed sixteenth century vault until their discovery by the amateur archaeologist John Edward Wilson-Claridge (1905–1993).

At the time, the Abbey site was owned by the Claridge family, a situation which enabled Wilson-Claridge to excavate the abbey ruins, culminating in his uncovering of the relics in 1931:

On 22 January it was decided to excavate between the memorial tablet stones...at a depth of only ten inches a large flat 'bedding stone' with its mortared face upwards was found resting upon four other stones, three of which were faced, but all of which were of uneven size. On the removal of the 'bedding' or covering stone, a tiny vault was disclosed, completely filled by a small lead casket.[47]

Part of the central portion of the lid of the casket had perished,but on lifting it Wilson-Claridge discovered that the casket contained human remains. The skeleton was incomplete, but the relatively small size of the casket (50 x 25 x 15 cm) indicated that it had been used for a reburial.

---

[46] The eleventh century bishop Wulfstan of York in his *Sermo Lupi ad Anglos* mentions, in passing, that the relics had been burned, but his version of events is not corroborated by any other source. It seems hard to credit that the bishop was speaking literally, given that Saint Edward's relics had been translated to Shaftesbury decades before. Possibly the bishop was alluding to the Scriptural verse: 'though I bestow all my goods to feed the poor, and though I give my body to be burned, and have not charity, it profiteth me nothing' (1. Cor. 13:3).

[47] J. Wilson-Claridge, *Report of Excavations on the site of the Royal Abbey Church of Our Lady & St. Eadward the Martyr at Shaftesbury AD 1930-31* (London: British Publishing Company Limited, 1932) p. 6

Inclement weather and failing light brought a halt to the work; the casket, with the relics inside, was left undisturbed inside the vault. The excavations were re-commenced on 24 January in the presence of Church of England representatives and a correspondent from the London *Times* who reports:

> *I was present on Saturday afternoon with a small company who were privileged to see the discovery which has now, it is believed, set at rest the speculation of centuries... The discovery is regarded as one of great importance. The casket itself is of unique interest, and totally unlike any other of the same period which has been used for the disposal of human remains. The lid was roughly shaped and the casket was made by rolling the corners into a scroll. The whole of the circumstances point to these remains being those of the murdered king.*[48]

The fourteenth century chapel which contained the shrine to Saint Edward was built in the space between the north transept and chancel with a flight of stairs leading down to the crypt (see photograph on page 64). It was whilst excavating around the top of the stairs that Wilson-Claridge made his discovery. The report of the Royal Commission on Historical Monuments describes the location:

> *Entrance to the crypt was by a canted flight of stairs... A roughly made leaden casket was unearthed in 1931 from a position which would correspond with the threshold of this entry; it contained the fractured bones of a young man, plausibly identified with the relics of St. Edward, perhaps reburied here in haste at the Dissolution. The upper chapel may thus be identified as that of St. Edward; presumably it contained a shrine to which the relics were translated in the 14th century.*[49]

---

[48] From our correspondent, 'Edward King and Martyr', *Times*, 26 Jan 1931 p. 8

[49] Royal Commission on Historical Monuments, *An Inventory of Historical Monuments in the County of Dorset*, pp. 58-59

Examinations of the Relics

The skeleton discovered by Wilson-Claridge was incomplete; this is to be expected given that relics of Saint Edward had been distributed widely. In 1962, Wilson-Claridge allowed the bones to be examined by Thomas Stowell CBE, FRCS, a consultant trauma surgeon. Stowell deduced, from the presence of greenstick fractures, that the bones were those of a young man.

In his report, he refers to a post-mortem he had performed following an industrial accident. The seventeen year old victim had been caught by his right foot in the driving-belt of a lathe. The power of the machine had dragged him up into the air and around the pulley above, causing injuries which later proved fatal.[50] Stowell notes that the fractures on the relics resembled those he had previously observed on the accident victim. He concludes: 'the bones show a concatenation of fractures which precisely fit the story of the murder. I cannot think of any other series of violences which could have produced this sequence of fractures.'[51]

In addition to Stowell's work, an osteological investigation was carried out at Wilson-Claridge's request by Don Brothwell of the British Museum. Brothwell concluded that the bones were those of a man between 25–35 and were therefore not those of Saint Edward.

Osteology involves analysing certain bone structures that are known to change with age. It is thought that these structures can function as age indicators by comparing them to those on a reference population of skeletons of known age. These skeletal age indicators are difficult to identify so any osteological investigation is highly subjective by nature.

There is, of course, no documented reference population for the Anglo-Saxon period; osteologists therefore use a more

---

[50] T. E. A. Stowell, 'The bones of Edward the Martyr' *The Criminologist*, Vol. 5 Nos. 16/17 (1970) p. 110

[51] *Ibid.* p. 119

modern population for reference and assume that the two populations have similar rates and patterns of skeletal change. They also assume that biological age correlates with chronological age within each population.

Biological age is affected by variables such as illness, diet and genetics. Some adults mature quickly and some more slowly. Skeletal age indicators, therefore, indicate biological age but not necessarily chronological age in years. By assuming a steady rate of ageing, osteological investigations tend to overestimate the age of young adults, and underestimate the age of older adults.[52]

There are also issues with the Harmann-Todd Osteological Collection used as a reference by osteologists in the 1970s. Many of the bodies in the collection were those of unclaimed, undocumented vagrants whose age at death was estimated, in many cases, by undertakers or mortuary attendants.[53] A technique that uses estimated ages in order to estimate ages is obviously unreliable.

Brothwell was an experienced and well-regarded osteologist, but his conclusion cannot be regarded as definitive. In fact, a widely-cited analysis found no statistically significant correlation between chronological age and the osteological age indicators used by Brothwell.[54]

Osteological investigations can only provide indications of broad stages of life. They are certainly not accurate or precise enough to disprove that the relics found by Wilson-Claridge are those of Saint Edward.

---

[52] J. Buckberry, 'The (mis)use of adult age estimates in osteology' *Annals of Human Biology*, Vol. 42 No.4 (2015) p. 328

[53] J. L. Muller, K. E. Pearlstein, C. de la Cova, 'Dissection and documented skeletal collections: embodiments of legalized inequality' in K. C. Nystrom (ed.) *The bioarchaelogy of dissection and autopsy in the United States* (Cham: Springer International Publishing Switzerland, 2017) p. 195

[54] J. P. Bocquet-Appel, C. Massett, Farewell to Paleodemography *Journal of Human Evolution* Vol. 11 No.4 (1982) pp. 321-333

Shaftesbury: The newly opened vault as discovered on 22 January 1931. The upright bedding-stone at the rear of the vault originally rested on the uneven stone walls. The lid of the lead casket is clearly visible

Image from the Courtenay Arthur Ralegh Radford Collection. Reproduced courtesy of University of Exeter Special Collections Archives.

Shaftesbury: The open casket with the lead lid upright. Note the holes in the centre of the lid where the lead has perished. Photograph taken before the relics were removed on 24 January 1931.

Image from the Courtenay Arthur Ralegh Radford Collection. Reproduced courtesy of University of Exeter Special Collections Archives.

Examination of the Casket

The casket in which the relics were found was examined in 1974 by the archeologist Ralegh Radford, a member of the Royal Commission on Historical Monuments.

In his report Radford notes that the casket had been formed from two lead sheets roughly twisted together; the edges of the sheets were unfinished and not soldered. The edges of the base sheet had been drawn up to form the sides of the casket, and the edges of the lid folded over forming a flange to fit over the sides. The lead used had been cut out of a larger piece formed of several sheets soldered together.

Radford concluded that the type of lead used suggested the reuse of a small coffin or large relic holder; the thickness and finish of the sheets ruled out the possibility of roofing lead being used. The casket's construction and location strongly indicated that it had been used for the hasty reburial of important relics at the Dissolution.[55]

Some might argue that, even though the construction of the casket and the vault infer a hasty sixteenth century reburial, the remains might not necessarily be those of a tenth century saint. In 1989, however, a portion of the relics obtained by a Roman Catholic priest before Wilson-Claridge offered them to the Orthodox, was subjected to radiocarbon dating at the Harwell Laboratory, Oxford. The sample was dated with 68% probability to between AD 810 and AD 980 and 95% probability to between AD 680 and AD 1030.

It is certainly possible that Saint Edward's relics were concealed by the nuns of the Abbey. However, unlikely as it may sound, the relics may have been reburied at the order of the King's Commissioners. This appears to have happened to the remains of William of York, which were discovered in

---

[55] C. A. R. Radford, *Lead Container found at Shaftesbury* (Unpublished Manuscript, 1984) p. 1

1968; it is all the more likely in Saint Edward's case as he had been King of England.

Radford was familiar with both the Stowell and Brothwell reports, but regarded both as less convincing than the strong historical evidence. The opinion of one of the twentieth century's greatest archaeologists is not without weight: 'all the circumstances indicate that the bones recovered in 1931 were relics and it is difficult to imagine that they were other than the relics from the shrine of St Edward.'[56]

The Relics Dispute

Wilson-Claridge was an agnostic, but he was determined that the relics should be given a suitable enshrinement. He offered them to several Roman Catholic and Church of England bishops on the condition that, firstly, they should recognize the relics as those of Saint Edward and, secondly, that they should allow them to be venerated. None of the bishops were willing to agree to his second condition.

By this time Wilson-Claridge had emigrated to Malta, but before doing so he had deposited the relics in a bank vault for safekeeping. Eventually, Wilson-Claridge's wish to donate the relics came to the notice of the Orthodox. In 1977, Archimandrite Alexis (Pobjoy) entered into correspondence with him and, after a long negotiation, Wilson-Claridge offered the relics to the Orthodox Church.

At the time, Archimandrite Alexis belonged to the Russian Orthodox Church Abroad (ROCA) – the free part of the Russian Orthodox Church in the west not associated with the Communist-infiltrated Church in Russia.

Archimandrite Alexis informed the ROCA Synod of Bishops of Wilson-Claridge's offer, and the bishops, after

---

[56] C. A. R. Radford, *The Relics of St. Edward, King and Martyr* (Unpublished Manuscript, 1985) p. 10

examining the issues closely, decreed that Saint Edward should be formally added to the Orthodox Calendar of saints and that his relics should be venerated.[57]

In order to provide a suitable shrine for the relics, the newly formed King Edward Orthodox Trust (KEOT) entered negotiations to purchase two derelict cemetery chapels in Brookwood Cemetery, Surrey. The sale was completed in 1982, and on 18 March of the same year Saint Edward Brotherhood was founded. The former mortuary chapel was adapted to become the Brotherhood residence, and the Anglican chapel the Shrine Church of Saint Edward. The relics were scheduled to be enshrined on 16 September 1984.

However, on 10 September all those involved in organizing the enshrinement were served with a writ of summons to appear before the High Court. The plaintiff, Wilson-Claridge's brother, Colonel Geoffrey Claridge, asked the court to grant an injunction halting the enshrinement. He had, for many years, claimed a part ownership of the relics, and wanted them returned to Shaftesbury Abbey.

Unfortunately, Bishop Constantine, the ROCA bishop in London, backed Colonel Claridge's legal action despite the Synod's approval of the enshrinement. Metropolitan Philaret (now Saint Philaret of New York) had previously confirmed the Synod's position in a letter to Archimandrite Alexis dated 2 August 1984:

> *Those who oppose the reception of the relics of St. Edward and the very sanctity of the Saint would do well to consider that they are opposing the very grace of God Himself, for which sin the spiritual penalty will doubtless not be negligible.*

The case was scheduled to be heard before the Honourable Mr Justice Nourse of the High Court's Chancery Di-

---

[57] Bishop Gregory, Secretary of the Synod of Bishops, 'Concerning St. Edward' *Orthodox Life* Vol 33 No. 1 (1983) p. 10

vision on 13 September. The case, however, was postponed until the next day; during the delay, Archimandrite Alexis received a telegram from Metropolitan Philaret confirming the Synod's approval for the enshrinement in the light of Bishop Constantine's opposition.

The Metropolitan's clearly stated position impressed Justice Nourse who dismissed Bishop Constantine's objection to the enshrinement. He permitted the service to go ahead, but ruled that the relics should be returned to the bank vault until the legal case over ownership was resolved. He warned the plaintiff that the case would be complicated and lengthy, because a dispute over ownership of human remains was unique and without precedent.

The legal situation then became more complicated with the involvement of the Treasury Solicitor, who acts for the Attorney General, the Crown's chief legal officer. On 26 April 1985 he notified KEOT's solicitor that the Crown had a substantial right and interest in the proper custody of the relics and as a consequence they should immediately be released into his custody. The Attorney General further instructed the Treasury Solicitor that, if the relics were not surrendered, legal proceedings should be started to ensure that the relics were kept in a place and manner satisfactory to the Crown.

It should be noted that, in the United Kingdom, the power of the Crown is vested in the monarch, but its functions are exercised by government ministers accountable only to parliament. In other words, ministers can act on the Crown's behalf without needing the approval of the monarch.

This separation between monarch and government is clearly demonstrated in the relics dispute. At no time since their discovery in 1931 had the Royal Family laid claim to the relics of Saint Edward. Prince Philip, the Duke of

Edinburgh (the husband of Queen Elizabeth II), had actual-ly already donated to the appeal to establish a Shrine Church for Saint Edward the Martyr.[58]

Colonel Geoffrey Claridge died in October 1986, but his death did not bring an end to the legal dispute. In a second High Court hearing on 25 April 1988, Deputy Judge Rob-ert A. K. Wright ruled that Colonel Claridge's daughter could continue the legal action and also confirmed the Attorney General as a party to the case. Significantly, the Attorney General's counsel clarified that the Crown held a neutral posi-tion on the question of the ownership of the relics, and was now only concerned with their safety and security.

The judge ruled that the relics could be returned to the Brotherhood if measures recommended in a report prepared by security consultant Stuart McAinsh on the instructions of the Treasury Solicitor's Office were implemented. However, the question of the ownership of the relics was not resolved at this hearing, and the case remained open.

On 14 December 1988, the Office of the Treasury Solici-tor informed the Brotherhood that the security measures had been approved, subject to a final inspection to be carried out by the security consultant.

The relics were returned to the Orthodox Church on 21 December 1988, the eve of both the Conception of the The-otokos and the commemoration of Saint Æthelgifu the first Abbess of Shaftesbury and daughter of King Alfred the Great.

Eventually, on 31 March 1995, the feast of the martyr-dom of Saint Edward (18 March on the Church Calendar), the Chancery Division of the High Court of Justice dismissed the case.

---

[58] Prince Philip's mother, Princess Alice of Battenburg (1885-1969) was Or-thodox. She became a nun in later life. See: Archbishop Chrysostomos, *A Greek Orthodox Nun in Buckingham Palace* (Etna: Centre for Traditionalist Orthodox Studies, 2003)

MIRACLES AND
ANSWERS TO PRAYER

I have also had some good news. Our Lord listened to my prayers and as a result, I received a letter from my son, which can only be a miracle. As you know, he left me and I hadn't had news of him for six years. What seems to be more than a coincidence is that his letter was dated 16th September, the very weekend of the enshrinement celebrations. What was amazing was his change of attitude towards me. He has invited me to visit him in America, and is prepared to pay for my ticket.

I. B. December 1984

I write in grateful thanks to Saint Edward for a prayer which was answered almost straightway. A friend's father was sent to hospital for tests with a suspected heart condition which had led to severe swelling and loss of appetite. The doctors were not hopeful as my friend's father had lost the will to live. The outlook was gloomy; furthermore the drugs prescribed were affecting his balance of mind and causing confusion. After listening to my friend's sad story, I prayed to Saint Edward for help. Within twenty-four hours, the patient was taken out of the oxygen tent and began to eat a little. The doctors reduced his drugs and little by little he improves daily to such an extent that he can now receive visitors; his mind is back to normal. Would you please pray for him at the service of Supplication to the Mother of God although he is not Orthodox.

P. D. September 1985

I used some of the holy oil you sent me, when I had a car accident. I anointed my leg with it, and to my surprise the pain vanished and my leg was fine. I have continued to try to have faith, and have been saying the canon to Saint Edward on a regular basis. God has been very merciful, and circumstances in my life have recently been very bearable. I am very grateful to Saint Edward for his intercessions.

A. F. March 1987

Edward is very well, thanks be to God. As I think I told you, we had some problems with the doctors in the pregnancy. My wife had caught the rare disease toxoplasmosis and the doctors wanted to abort him, which naturally we refused to do. According to them, he should have been blind! At birth, when I saw the umbilical cord, it was clear that the disease had stopped at the cord; this was quite visible, even to me. This was one of the original motivations for giving the name Edward, since the saint's first miracle was the healing of the blind woman. I cannot say that a miracle has happened with our son, but we personally believe it. Thanks be to God for all things!

Deacon A. P. March 1987

Your welcome letter is also a reminder and opportunity to keep a promise I made to Saint Edward last winter. You may recall that, while I was in Denver you sent, at my request, a small bottle of oil from his vigil lamp, as well as tissue in which his relics had been wrapped. Last winter our youngest daughter Faith – 9 years old – developed a small tumour on the upper gum of her mouth. It was removed but it grew back, and was again removed surgically and this time sent off to a lab for a biopsy. We were told, pending lab results, to prepare ourselves for the likelihood that it was a malignancy and could mean cancer. While we awaited the test results I began to pray fervently to Saint Edward, anointing Faith with the oil and touching the tissue to her mouth each day while invoking Saint Edward. I promised him that if the test results came back negative – or, if positive, if a healing took place – I would do everything in my power to spread further knowledge of and devotion to him. The test came back negative – it was a benign tumour – but we told it would probably continue to grow back. However, thanks to his intercession, it didn't, and there's been no further difficulty whatever. So, I've both talked to many and written to others about our gratefully received little miracles and I take this opportunity to let you know, too. I don't know if you keep chronicles or records such answered prayers, but if so I want to include this testimony in your archives for the saint.

Priest A. Y. October 1991

I heard the following from a Bulgarian named Edward whom I met at the Holy Sepulchre on Great Friday. The man had not been baptized as a child, and he had recently asked an Orthodox priest in Jerusalem to baptise him. The priest agreed, but asked Edward to choose a new name because the name 'Edward' was not Orthodox. The night before the baptism a young man wearing a purple cloak and a square shaped golden crown appeared to Edward and said 'I am Edward, King of the English. You bear my name. Be baptised.' On hearing what had occurred I showed my friend Edward a small icon of St. Edward that I carry with me. He recognized the saint at once. When he heard about the vision the priest realised that he had made a mistake and baptised the man with the name 'Edward.'

R. S. 1997

I was suffering from terrible pains in my left eye. Nothing helped me, and all the specialists agreed that surgery was going to do more damage than help. One night, when I woke up from intense pains in my left eye, I, without thinking what and why I am doing it, started to search for a tiny piece of cotton, which was given me at Saint Edward's Brotherhood.

I found it and put it on my left eye. I called upon Saint Edward with a short prayer and immediately went to sleep. In the morning I thought 'what a strange thing I have done in the night'. I looked in the St. Herman calendar and realised that it was exactly Saint Edward's feast day - March 31! I thought, 'if only I would have asked them to remember me in a *molieben* [prayer service], my eye would have been healed completely. Since March 31 or, more precisely, April 1, I have never again suffered from the pains in my eye, although it has not healed completely. I am writing you because tomorrow is St. Edward's feast day.

L. J. October 2005

I'd like to tell you a short story connected with Saint Edward. In September 2006, I was to be operated on. Though it was a small operation on the toe, I was anxious and before it I had prayed in front of my icons at home. Then I took the icon of St. Edward and thought: 'How can you help me? You are not Russian etc.' When I came to the hospital it turned out that my doctor was Edward. The operation was successful. Thanks God.

Anon. May 2007

While standing in church during a Sunday Liturgy, I was suddenly overcome with excruciating back pain. It was so bad that I had to force other worshippers out of my way in the crowded church so that I could sit down, as I was worried I was about to collapse. After resting for a while, but still in considerable pain, I managed to make my way over to the Shrine of Saint Edward where I anointed my back with oil from the shrine lamp as best I could. Within about ten minutes, the pain had subsided completely and I was able to stand through the rest of the service.

A. B. 2019

I had a pain and blurred vision in my right eye and my optician took a picture behind the eye, and found a tear in the retina. I was sent to the hospital eye department, and they confirmed the result and put me on steroids, which didn't work. So they then sent me for an injection in my eye, which also didn't work. They said there was no more they could do! I told this to Fr A. and he told me to pray to Saint Edward the Martyr, which I did, and later dipped my finger into the oil lamp and put it on my forehead above the eye. The pain and blurred vision disappeared and I thanked Saint Edward for such a wonderful gift. I had a check-up with my own optician and he said that he had never seen a tear like mine, and yet I was still able to see. I didn't even have to change my glasses! He said, 'What a miracle!' And I replied, 'Yes, the power of prayer.' So you see how grateful I am to Fr S., telling me the story of Saint Edward's healing of eyes, and very grateful to Saint Edward.

B. W. July 2022

A parishioner who had returned to live in Australia sent us a report of a miracle of Saint Edward which was worked for a friend of hers. The friend was pregnant, but found that the pregnancy was ectopic. Doctors advised that for her own safety she should have an abortion. The woman, although an atheist, was deeply convinced that the life of the unborn was of worth and pregnancies should not be terminated. Our former parishioner gave her friend some oil from the vigil lamp of St Edward the Martyr at Brookwood, and told her to rub some on her stomach. Although she was an unbeliever, the woman was desperate and did so. The next time tests were made it was seen that the foetus had moved and was now properly developing in her womb and she gave birth to a healthy baby.

A. A. June 2023

John Wilson-Claridge presenting the relics of
Saint Edward the Martyr
September 1984

THE RECORDED MIRACLES OF ST EDWARD THE MARTYR

by
J. Wilson-Claridge
Hon. Director of Excavations at
Shaftesbury Abbey, Dorset
1930-1932

REVISED EDITION

First published in 1984 as ISBN: 0-947935-00-2

Preface to the Revised Edition

Some minor revisions have been made to the 1984 edition. Anglo-Saxon names now reflect current academic usage. Errata have been corrected and explanatory footnotes added. The photographs in the first edition have been replaced.

Wilson-Claridge was not Orthodox, and this is often obvious in his historical analysis, use of religious terminology and general tone. That having been said, *The Recorded Miracles of Saint Edward the Martyr* remains an important historical work by the finder and donor of the sacred relics.

Introduction

St Edward, son of prince Edgar by his first wife Æthelflæd, was born in the year 959, before his father inherited the throne, following the death of King Edwy, which occurred later in the same year. Edward's mother died, either at the time of his birth or very shortly afterwards. There is no record of the actual date of her death.

It is sometimes suggested that Edward was not born until 962, but this is clearly an error, as the principal objection to Edward's coronation was that neither his father nor his mother were crowned at the time of his birth, and we know that King Edgar succeeded to the throne in 959. In fact it was St Edward's half-sister Edith who was born in 962. She was the illegitimate daughter of King Edgar and the Lady Wulfthryth. It seems that King Edgar had promised to marry Wulfthryth, but did not do so.

We must therefore assume that Edgar was in a position to marry her some considerable time before her daughter was born and that consequently he was a widower when he proposed marriage. This fact is in accordance with the suggestion that Edward's mother did not long survive the birth of her son.

King Edgar died suddenly on July 8th 976, and was succeeded in the same month by his eldest son St Edward, whose
hurried coronation was arranged by Archbishop Dunstan and
the supporters of the monastic clergy in order to frustrate the
order of married clerics from regaining their authority, which
had been suppressed by King Edgar in favour of the celibate
monks of whom St Edward was a devout follower.

We will now pass to the consideration of the miracles at-
tributed to St Edward following his murder at Corfe Castle in
Dorset which took place at eventide on March 18th 979 (see
Glastonbury Abbey Easter Table for a contemporary record).[59]

The King's murder was undoubtedly committed by the
thanes of his step-brother Prince Æthelred. After they had
ridden out to meet King Edward and were waiting for his
arrival at the entrance to the village of Corfe, they planned
the details of the crime, which may have been suggested to
them by young Æthelred, who though only eight years old at
the time was not incapable of letting his thanes know that St
Edward stood between him and any chance of his succeeding
to the throne. At least it is significant that no one was ever
punished for the crime.

The Murder of Saint Edward

When St Edward arrived at the entrance to Corfe, he was
surrounded by the conspirators and was fatally stabbed. He
slipped from his saddle and was dragged, one foot caught in
the stirrup, until he finally fell lifeless into the small streams at
the base of the hill on which the castle of Corfe was later built,
the ruins of which still stand.

We are told by the writer William of Malmesbury (1127)
that Ælfthryth's servants took the King's body from the stream

---

[59] The construction of Corfe Castle began many decades after the martyrdom. Wilson-Claridge correctly points this out later in the text.

and placed it in a small cottage (presumably a one-roomed shack):

[This cottage] *was occupied by an old blind woman, whom Ælfthryth, out of her charity, maintained. The dead King's body was covered with a mean covering, but during the night, the room was filled with a strange light. The old woman recovered her sight and removing the covering realised that beneath it lay the body of the King.*

This was the first recorded miracle of St Edward; it may well be purely legendary, but in support of it, it is said that the Church of St Edward at Corfe stands on the site of the cottage where the King's body lay, and was dedicated to him from its earliest foundation.

Further, the stream at the base of the hill from which his body was lifted, was in after years, visited by pilgrims who washed their eyes in its water to regain or improve their sight. Even within the knowledge of the writer, two persons are reported to have performed this ablution of the eyes at this spot. This modern action supports the story of the blind woman having miraculously received the restoration of her sight, which was firmly believed down to the Middle Ages.

On the day following the murder of St Edward, his body was taken to the convent at Wareham and hurriedly buried outside the old Saxon conventual church, without any kingly honours.

From the chronicler John Brompton, we learn that from the burial place of the King a spring of fresh water burst forth, and that many people came there to seek healing for their ills, by prayer and by bathing in the holy water issuing from the grave of the King.[60]

---

[60] John Brompton was elected Abbot of Jervauix in 1436. The chronicle ascribed to him was written in the latter half of the fourteenth century. It is possible that Brompton is not the author, but merely ordered the copying of an anonymous manuscript.

The Translation of the Relics

As a result of the fame noised abroad by the many cures wrought at the place of the King's interment, it was decided to remove his body and translate it to the great Abbey of Shaftesbury for reburial in the thickness of the wall on the north side of the High Altar. From the chronicle of John Brompton, who unfortunately cannot be regarded as a strictly accurate authority, we learn that:

The illustrious Duke Ælfhere came with a multitude of people and ordered that the King's body should be taken up out of the ground. When this was done, they found him naked and saw that he was free from any corruption or decay. Then the attendants washed the body of the revered King, clothed it with new garments, and placed it in a chest or coffin, and noble soldiers, placing the bier upon their shoulders, carried him to a place where he was buried with all honour.

It is interesting to note here that it is certain that until the fourteenth century, when it was burnt down, a small wooden Saxon church stood at the east end of the present church of St Mary, which covered the site of St Edward's original interment.

During this first translation of St Edward we are told, again by Brompton:

That two poor men, doubled up by rheumatism, so that they were unable to walk, crawled beneath the bier, praying that they might be cured of their affliction through the merits of the holy saint and as a result of their faith they were instantly cured.

This statement of Brompton is unsupported in the records of any other authority and I fear should not be regarded too seriously.

There is also a well-known story, without contemporary verification, that Ælfthryth, who had intended to follow the cortege on horseback, was unable to do so as her horse refused to proceed, and that even when she decided to follow the bier on foot, she was forcibly prevented from doing so by unseen hands. This story was recorded many years later by those who thought that she was privy to Edward's murder.

The certainty that she did not attend the translation is far more likely to have been due to the probability of her being far from Wareham at the time; she was indeed almost sure to have been in Winchester with her young son King Æthelred, or at least with him at one of his many manors. Or indeed, that she was unwilling to attend the translation because it was led by Archbishop Dunstan, whom she had very good reasons for disliking and despising since he had done all in his power to get her to dissolve her marriage to King Edgar, calling her an adulteress because she had married a man who was, almost certainly, responsible for the death of her former husband, the Earl of Athelwood.

After King Edward's body had been carried to Shaftesbury, in what was probably the greatest religious procession ever to have taken place in Dorset (which according to the Abbess, Elizabeth Shelford, required seven days to complete, starting on February 13th 981, and arriving at Shaftesbury Abbey on February 20th), it was placed in the grave prepared for it near the high altar.[61]

There is no doubt that at the time of this translation Edward was already recognised as a saint on account of his murder and the many miracles attributed to him. For the next twenty years, St Edward lay in his grave, the object of pilgrimage and veneration, after which time it was decided to enshrine his relics in a costly and elaborate shrine.

---

[61] Wilson-Claridge's source *Elizabeth Shelford's Book of Hours* (Fitzwilliam MS. 2 1957) dates the *adventus* at Shaftesbury to 18 February, not 20 February. See: Simon Keynes, 'King Alfred the Great and Shaftesbury Abbey' in Laurence Keen (ed.) *Studies in the History of Shaftesbury Abbey* (Dorchester, 1999) p. 58

We are told that this decision resulted from the continual slight levitation of the cover of his grave, and from the dreams of a devout man to whom St Edward is said to have appeared and indicated that he wished to lie in his tomb no longer. It seems that this man went to the Abbess and told her of his dreams. The Abbess referred the matter to King Æthelred, who ordered the lifting up of St Edward's relics and their enshrinement in a suitable place in the Abbey Church.

The Glorification of Saint Edward

Although St Edward was undoubtedly regarded as a saint from the time of his translation from Wareham, he was not officially canonized until 1008, by an act of the All-England Council under the Holy Martyr Ælfheah, Archbishop of Canterbury.

There is in existence a charter by St Edward's step-brother King Æthelred, dated 1001 (the date of Edward's enshrinement), which clearly states:

I, King Æthelred, King of the English, with humble prayer, offer the monastery, which is commonly called Bradford, to Christ and to his Saint, namely my brother Edward, whom the Lord himself deigns to exalt in our days by many signs of virtue, after his blood was shed.

This historical document proves that King Æthelred recognised that his brother was a saint exalted by God (through his many signs of virtue), at least as early as St Edward's enshrinement or uplifting on June 20th 1001.

It indeed seems that by this date the Relics of St Edward had become so famous owing to the many miracles attributed to his intercession that his name was added to the original dedication of the Abbey, which was to the Virgin Mary, so that from the time of his enshrinement, the convent was generally known as St Edward's Abbey, while the ancient town of

Shaftesbury, was for hundreds of years, called Edwardstowe or in official documents *Burgus Sancti Edwardi.*

Surely the great importance of St Edward's relics proves beyond question that many strange and unaccountable cures must have been wrought at his shrine. In the chronicle of John Brompton, which is endorsed by other ancient chroniclers, he states:

> *In the year 1001 after the incarnation of Our Lord, when now the merits of the glorious martyr Edward, brother of King Æthelred, were made known far and wide by the mighty and wonderful cures, which daily were done at his tomb, that when the tomb was opened with the greatest reverence, so fragrant an odour rose from it, that all those who were there thought that they were standing in the delights of paradise.*

The chronicler follows this somewhat exaggerated statement (indeed the fragrance might have been due to the still lingering odours of the herbs and ointments with which the King's body was anointed at the time of his first burial in the abbey church) by recording that

> *The Bishops reverently approached and raised the sacred relics from the tomb, composing them carefully in a place of honour, made ready for the purpose. Thus the sacred body was uplifted in the twenty-first year after it was buried.* [That is from February 18th 981 to June 20th 1001, a period of twenty years and four months.] *Later some part of the relics were removed to Leofmonasterium* [Leominster] *and some to Abenonia* [Abingdon]. *The place in Siptonia* [Shaftesbury] *where his lung still palpitates with undiminished virtue is called Edwardstowe.*

Note: that part of Shaftesbury to the west of the town centre, which was occupied by the abbey church, the conventual buildings and the Abbey parks covered eleven acres and is still called Edwardstowe.

Early Recorded Miracles

The above detailed account of the enshrinement of St Edward by Brompton proves that, at the time that he wrote his chronicle, the relics of the young King were firmly established as a means of Divine Grace through faith and supplication at his shrine, not in a remote past, but at a time contemporary with the author.

There is no doubt that faith in the virtues of St Edward was universal in England. King Æthelred ordered that the three feast days of St Edward should be celebrated in the whole church throughout England, while Polydore Virgil states that 'many miracles then happened, so that Saint Edward was rightly reckoned amongst divine beings.'

Some further references to the miracles of St Edward were recorded by an unknown monk, probably a member of the Chapter at Abingdon during the eleventh century. Although the writer appears to have had access to earlier records, I am referring here only to those miracles which seem to have taken place in the eleventh century when the unknown monk was apparently still alive and of which he may have had actual knowledge, or access to such knowledge. The writer states that

A man called John, who lived in North West France, whose whole body was bent with pains so that his heels were touching his loins and he was unable to stand upright, nor had he any use of his legs, was said to have had a vision, that he should go to England to the Abbey of Shaftesbury where St Edward was enshrined and that there he would recover his health. With the help of his neighbours and kin he crossed the Channel and at last reached the Abbey. There having prayed to God and to St Edward, he recovered his health and was restored to wholeness and he then remained in the Convent as a servant till the end of his life, whilst all those persons who saw him bare witness to the miracle to this day.

In a further instance of divine assistance, resulting in a cure, the unknown monk states that

A leper came to the tomb of St Edward and when he invoked divine help in prayer and vigils, for his infirmity, he was cleansed from all defilement of his leprosy. Yet another miracle followed this, after an interval, through the same worshipful saint, of which we learn through reliable people who saw it. The venerable Heremann, bishop of the church at Salisbury, was on one occasion journeying around the parishes of his diocese. He had turned aside to visit the convent at Shaftesbury, when a poor man, whom he used to support out of charity, came forward in his retinue. This man, who was blind and who was led by a boy who guided his steps, entered the church to pray, where he remained till evening, begging God's help for his disablement; when the church wardens found him, they urged him to leave, but he declared that he would not, he would wait upon the mercy of God and of St Edward. So, being impressed by his faith, they allowed him to lie there in prayer, but made the boy return to his lodgings; for some time the man remained there quietly after which he recovered his sight. When this was made known in the morning, those of sound mind could not easily be persuaded to believe it, until those who knew the man before were questioned and as witnesses of the truth affirmed that he had been blind for a long time; then at the bishop's bidding a crowd of people assembled in the church and with the nuns serving God, they paid homage to Christ who thought fit to honour the merits of St Edward.

After this another man, who had been bound in heavy iron chains, because of his sins [he was apparently mentally ill], *earnestly prayed in the same church, the more urgently on account of the pain of his fetters; they were broken and fell off and he won his freedom by the merits of the man of God, St Edward. Many other miracles were performed through St Edward's merits, but those were scarcely recorded in writing.*

The importance of this record of miracles lies in the fact that they can presumably be dated to the early 11th century, or to that period when the writer was himself alive and that therefore he probably had first-hand knowledge of them. I have omitted any miracles recorded prior to the latter years of the reign of King Edward the Confessor, as the unknown monk certainly could not vouch for their authenticity.

Turning to the twelfth century, there is one remarkable miracle, which is recorded by William of Malmesbury and also in the *Monasticon Anglicanum* which follows that writer; it states, and I quote: 'The place at Shaftesbury where his (St. Edward's) lung still quivers with undiminished animation is called Edwardstow.'[62]

Elsewhere we read that when William of Malmesbury visited the Abbey in about 1135 he actually saw the miraculous lung. It is impossible to understand this extraordinary preservation of the lung. It seems certain that the relics of the saint were not exposed to public view in their shrine, any more than were the relics of other famous saints. We must therefore conclude that the lung had been removed from the rest of the relics and placed elsewhere where it could be seen if necessary by very important persons.

In this connection, I must record here that an eleventh century Saxon glass vessel, or vase, was found in 1904, beneath a small marble slab in the centre of the footpace in front of the High Altar.[63] This discovery was made during the excavation of that part of the church by Mr Doran Webb, whose report states that, 'when found it contained a shrunken nut like object.' Mr Doran Webb suggested that the object was possibly the heart of King Canute, simply, it would seem, on the basis that Canute was known to have died in Shaftesbury.

[62] The *Monasticon Anglicanum* by Sir William Dugdale is a history of English monasticism published in 1693.

[63] A 'footpace' is a raised platform or dais.

Mr Doran Webb ignored the fact that there is no record of Canute bestowing his heart to Shaftesbury before his burial in Winchester, nor indeed was there any reason why he should have done so. However, Mr Doran Webb presented his find to the then owner of the Abbey site who had given permission for the excavation to take place.

Some years later, the glass vase or pot was presented to the Chapter at Winchester Cathedral, where it may still be seen, but the relic it contained was thrown away when the vase or pot was handed over to the church authorities. Is it not possible, or indeed likely, that this vase actually contained the withered lung of St Edward? Where else, other than before the High Altar, would the Abbess and Convent have placed so sacred an object, and indeed how simple it would have been for William of Malmesbury or any other celebrity to see the miraculous lung simply by raising the small marble slab. My horror at the throwing away of this precious object is beyond my powers of expression.

I will now pass rapidly down the centuries, pausing only to note a few references, which clearly indicate that until the dissolution, the repercussions of which ended forever the story of the majority of our great monastic houses, the Relics of St Edward remained an object of great veneration and importance.

Shaftesbury: Fifteenth century Cross reset on a stone plinth in 1931. Situated on the site of the Norman High Altar.

It is recorded that amongst the greatest of the pilgrims to the shrine of St Edward was the Danish King Canute, who visited the Abbey on a number of occasions and died, almost certainly, in the Abbey church, on the 12th November 1035.

In 1317, Bishop Roger of Salisbury granted forty-one days indulgence on the days of the translation and forty days on the passion of St Edward. In 1412 an indulgence was granted to all those who visited the threshold of the saint. Later Archbishop Chicheley directed that the feasts of St Edward should be observed with double offices.

There are many references to the relics of Edward in letters from the Convent to the Crown; thus in 1382, in a petition to the King when the abbey was vacant owing to the death of the Abbess Jean Fermage, the following words occur: 'May it please you, by the love of God and his sweet mother, St Mary, and of the glorious heart of St Edward the Martyr, your noble progenitor, who in your said house lies canonised' etc., etc.

The Discovery of the Relics

As it is not my intention here to deal with matters other than those associated with the miracles of St Edward, I will pass over the desecration of the Abbey; suffice it to say here that the relics of St Edward were not destroyed. His shrine was stripped of all its ornamentation and wealth, but his bones were removed from the shrine and hidden in a remote corner of the church, in the same manner as were those of St Wilfrid of York, which were removed from his desecrated shrine and hidden beneath a stone slab in the nave of the great church.

St Edward's bones were discovered in their hiding place in the North Transept of the abbey church and later were taken by the eminent osteologist Mr T.E.A. Stowell and minutely examined, both as to the actual age and sex of the individual whose bones they were and further as to the cause of the numerous injuries manifest in them, which corresponded exactly with the circumstances of the King's murder, while the missing bones from the remains doubtlessly were accounted for by those donated and sent as relics to Abingdon and Shrewsbury and possibly other religious foundations.

All the details of Mr Stowell's brilliant and painstaking examination are contained in my manuscript 'The Life of Saint Edward' which still awaits publication, but Mr Stowell's report has already been published in Vol. 5, Nos. 16/17 of *The Criminologist* for May/August 1970. Mr Stowell concludes his report by stating: 'I cannot escape the conviction, on historical, anatomical and surgical grounds that beyond all reasonable doubt, we have here the bones of St Edward, King and Martyr.'

Shaftesbury: Steps leading from the crypt to the Chapel of Saint Edward; the relics were discovered on the threshold of the chapel. Photograph probably taken during the excavations of 1931.

It was not very long after Mr Stowell issued his report on the relics, that I took up residence in Malta, having placed the sacred bones in the vaults of a bank for safe keeping. With the subsequent death of my old friend and collaborator the final disposal of the relics was left in abeyance.

I had negotiated with the Abbot of Buckfast, with the Bishop of Winchester, the Bishop of Exeter and with the Roman Catholic Bishop of Plymouth. All the details of these negotiations can be found in my manuscript on St Edward.

All of these ecclesiastics were willing to receive the relics, but they all declined to agree that the relics should be enshrined and made available for prayer and reverence, particularly on the appointed feast days of the saint. This both Mr Stowell and I insisted on and therefore in each case correspondence with the various parties was discontinued.

I must admit that I felt that just as Mr Stowell had appeared without being sought by me and made his masterly scientific examination of the relics, so, sooner or later, some unexpected solution would materialise and a suitable resting place for them would be found where they would receive the veneration to which they were entitled.

My faith was not misplaced; eventually as a result of a visit to the site of the abbey ruins by a member of the Russian Orthodox Church in Exile, I received a request for any available information I had on St Edward's relics. I at once sent this gentleman a copy of my 'History of Shaftesbury Abbey', my report on the two years' excavations on the Abbey site, as carried out by me; a copy of the detailed examination of the relics by Mr T.E.A. Stowell, and also a report by the eminent archaeologist Mr Ralegh Radford on his detailed examination of the casket in which the remains were found.

All these reports were later forwarded to the Orthodox bishops in America, who placed them before their Synod. As a result the Synod was enthusiastic for the relics to be received and enshrined in a church specially purchased for their reception at Brookwood near Woking.

Work for the alterations of this church, to meet the requirements of the Orthodox Brotherhood, and the erection of a shrine is nearing completion and it is anticipated that very shortly the relics will be received and enshrined by one or more bishops of the church.

Thus, without any approach by me, St Edward is at last to receive a resting place and veneration among a Communion whose doctrine is far closer to that which he knew in his lifetime, than either that of the present Church of Rome, or the reformed Church of England. One is left to wonder what power directed the priest of the Orthodox Church to visit Shaftesbury and start the negotiations, which have led to this overwhelmingly satisfactory conclusion.

Appendix

Some strange happenings on the Abbey site and recent cures through faith and supplication to St Edward within my knowledge.

1. No person has died in the Abbey House or the Abbey Lodge, during the last 150 years. Unfortunately I have no records on this point beyond 1830.

2. A Roman Catholic lady who visited the site confirmed that while doing so she heard the singing of nuns on the site of the Abbey quire and that she remained there for some time after the singing ceased. Perhaps this was simply an illusion on her part, due to her strong faith and her reverence for the holy site, but there is further evidence to support her statement: a young air force officer and his wife, who were living in the Abbey Lodge for a short time during the last war, stated that they had heard singing and chanting on the site,

on two occasions, at midnight, but that on looking out over the grounds, they had seen nothing to account for it. These two young persons had no strong attachment to any church.

3. My maternal grandmother, who was living with us at the Abbey House (having been brought there ostensibly to die after her discharge from hospital, as she was suffering from an inoperable illness), asked me if prayers for her recovery could be offered to St Edward at the Roman Catholic church of St Edward in Shaftesbury. I approached the priest in charge of the church, a certain Father Donsi (the predecessor of the present incumbent), and asked him if he would consider doing this for a lady who was not a member of his communion; he most kindly agreed and on the following Sunday he prayed earnestly for St Edward's intercession, that she might be cured of her malady. Within a few days she had completely recovered. She subsequently bought herself a house in Shaftesbury and lived in it for nearly ten years, dying eventually of old age in her 79th or 80th year. I should perhaps add that Father Donsi had complete faith in the healing relics of "his little saint" as he always called St Edward.

There is another record of a miraculous happening, of which I have first-hand knowledge. I was working on the Abbey site, when a lady approached me and asked if she might see the relics. I took her into the small temporary chapel in the Abbey House, where she knelt down in silent prayer for some considerable time in front of the relics, which were encased in a wooden container and visible through its glass front. After leaving the chapel, she thanked me and departed. The following day I was surprised to see her in Shaftesbury Market. She approached me and said:

I suppose that you are wondering why I prayed for so long to St Edward, before his relics. I live in Gillingham - [about 4 miles distant from Shaftesbury]; *my mother was dying of dropsy and was not expected to survive more than a few days. I came to St Edward to pray for my mother's recovery through his intercession. When I returned to Gillingham I found that she was completely recovered.*

The lady left me without telling me her name and I never saw her again, but I believe that she told me the truth, although I cannot confirm it.

The above four strange records are within my personal knowledge. I must leave it to the reader to draw his own conclusions concerning them.

The following short prayer, taken from the Sarum Breviaries under the heading 'Martyrdom', concludes this short essay on the miracles of St. Edward.

O God, conqueror of everlasting power, look favourably upon thy family, now celebrating the martyrdom of King Edward, and grant that, as thou dost deign to glorify him with Heavenly reward, so you may make us, under his protection, worthy to be assigned eternal felicity, through Jesus Christ our Lord.

Historical Information

Translations of the Anglo-Saxon Chronicles A.B.C.D.
The Book of Hours by Elizabeth Shelford
The Chartulary of Shaftesbury Abbey
The Chronicle of John Brompton
Old English History, by William Camden
Chronicle of John Wallingford
The History of the English by Geoffrey Gairner
English Historical Documents
The Chronicle of Roger de Hovendon
History of the Kings of England, by Simon of Durham
Life of Dunstan, by Osbert, written in the 12th century
Life of Dunstan, by Osbern, written about 1070
The *Monasticon Anglicorum*
The History of the English Kings
The *Vita Sancta Oswaldi*, by a monk of Ramsey Abbey
The works of Wulfstan, Nom de plume - The Wulf
An 11th century unknown Monk
The Writer of Worcester
Flores Historiarum, by Roger of Wendover

Modern Works Consulted

The *Acta Sanctorum*
Anglo-Saxon England, by Sir Frank Stenton
The Monastic Book of England, by Michael Alford
The Making of England, by John Richard Green
Church Decoration & Symbolism, by The Rev. E. Geldert
Butler's Lives of the Saints
Arthur's Britain, by Leslie Alcock
Report on the Relics of St. Edward, by T.E.A. Stowell
Report on St. Edward's Lead Casket, by Dr. C.S. Ralegh Radford

Principal Feasts of Saint Edward the Martyr According to the Julian Calendar

18 March: Martyrdom of the holy Passion-bearer.
3 September: Enshrinement of the relics at Brookwood.

SUPPLICATORY CANON TO SAINT EDWARD THE MARTYR

The priest: Blessed is our God, always now and ever, and unto the ages of ages.

The reader: Amen.

Glory to Thee, our God, glory to Thee.

Heavenly King, O Comforter, the Spirit of truth, Who art everywhere present and fillest all things, O Treasury of every good and Bestower of life: come and dwell in us, and cleanse us from every stain, and save our souls, O Good One.

Holy God, Holy Mighty, Holy Immortal, have mercy on us. (*thrice*)

Glory to the Father, and to the Son, and to the Holy Spirit; both now and ever, and unto the ages of ages. Amen.

All-holy Trinity, have mercy on us. Lord, be gracious unto our sins. Master, pardon our iniquities. Holy One, visit and heal our infirmities for Thy Name's sake.

Lord, have mercy. (*thrice*)

Glory to the Father, and to the Son, and to the Holy Spirit, both now and ever, and unto the ages of ages. Amen.

Our Father, Which art in the heavens, hallowed be Thy Name. Thy kingdom come. Thy will be done, on earth as it is in Heaven. Give us this day our daily bread. And forgive us our debts, as we forgive our debtors. And lead us not into temptation, but deliver us from the evil one.

The priest: For Thine is the kingdom, and the power, and the glory, of the Father, and of the Son, and of the Holy Spirit, now and ever, and unto the ages of ages.

The reader: Amen. Lord, have mercy (*twelve times).* Glory to the Father, and to the Son, and to the Holy Spirit; both now and ever, and unto the ages of ages. Amen.

O come, let us worship and fall down before our King and God.

O come, let us worship and fall down before Christ, our King and God.

O come, let us worship and fall down before Him, Christ the King and our God.

PSALM 142

O Lord, hear my prayer, give ear unto my supplication in Thy truth; hearken unto me in Thy righteousness.

And enter not into judgment with Thy servant, for in Thy sight shall no man living be justified.

For the enemy hath persecuted my soul; he hath humbled my life down to the earth.

He hath sat me in darkness as those that have been long dead, and my spirit within me is become despondent; within me my heart is troubled.

I remembered days of old, I meditated on all Thy works, I pondered on the creations of Thy hands.

I stretched forth my hands unto Thee; my soul thirsteth after Thee like a waterless land.

Quickly hear me, O Lord; my spirit hath fainted away.

Turn not Thy face away from me, lest I be like unto them that go down into the pit.

Cause me to hear Thy mercy in the morning; for in Thee have I put my hope.

Cause me to know, O Lord, the way wherein I should walk; for unto Thee have I lifted up my soul.

Rescue me from mine enemies, O Lord; unto Thee have I fled for refuge.

Teach me to do Thy will, for Thou art my God.

Thy good Spirit shall lead me in the land of uprightness; for Thy Name's sake, O Lord, shalt Thou quicken me.

In Thy righteousness shalt Thou bring my soul out of affliction, and in Thy mercy shalt Thou utterly destroy mine enemies. And Thou shalt cut off all them that afflict my soul, for I am Thy servant.

And straightway God is the Lord *is chanted:*

Fourth Tone

God is the Lord, and hath appeared unto us; blessed is He that cometh in the Name of the Lord.

And the same is also chanted after each verse:

Verse: O give thanks unto the Lord, and call upon His holy Name.

Verse: All the nations compassed me round about, and by the Name of the Lord I warded them off.

Verse: This is the Lord's doing, and it is marvellous in our eyes.

Then the following Troparia:

Fourth Tone

Thou who wast raised up

Thou strovest valiantly O martyred King Edward * against all those who opposed the monastics * when thou didst govern righteously and piously. * We the faithful honour thee * as our fervent protector * and with faith we venerate * thine all-hon'rable relics * whilst ever loudly singing with one voice: * O Passion-bearer save all by thy holy prayers.

Glory.

As one bestowed by God with power of healing * to cure all manner of sickness and suffering * do thou O Martyr Edward hearken unto us. * Heal all those who have recourse * with pure faith to thy relics * heeding unto their requests * that are unto salvation * and do thou strengthen those who strive to be * genuine Orthodox Christians in ev'ry deed.

Both now.

O Theotokos, we shall not cease from speaking * of all thy mighty acts, all we the unworthy ones; * for if thou hadst not stood to intercede for us, * who would have delivered us * from such numerous dangers? * Who would have preserved us all * until now in true freedom? * O Lady, we shall not turn away from thee; * for thou dost always save thy servants from all manner of grief.

PSALM 50

Have mercy on me, O God, according to Thy great mercy; and according to the multitude of Thy compassions blot out my transgression.

Wash me thoroughly from mine iniquity, and cleanse me from my sin.

For I know mine iniquity, and my sin is ever before me.

Against Thee only have I sinned and done this evil before Thee, that Thou mightest be justified in Thy words, and prevail when Thou art judged.

For behold, I was conceived in iniquities, and in sins did my mother bear me.

For behold, Thou hast loved truth; the hidden and secret things of Thy wisdom hast Thou made manifest unto me.

Thou shalt sprinkle me with hyssop, and I shall be made clean; Thou shalt wash me, and I shall be made whiter than snow.

Thou shalt make me to hear joy and gladness; the bones that be humbled, they shall rejoice.

Turn Thy face away from my sins, and blot out all mine iniquities.

Create in me a clean heart, O God, and renew a right spirit within me.

Cast me not away from Thy presence, and take not Thy Holy Spirit from me.

Restore unto me the joy of Thy salvation, and with Thy governing Spirit establish me.

I shall teach transgressors Thy ways, and the ungodly shall turn back unto Thee.

Deliver me from blood-guiltiness, O God, Thou God of my salvation; my tongue shall rejoice in Thy righteousness.

O Lord, Thou shalt open my lips, and my mouth shall declare Thy praise.

For if Thou hadst desired sacrifice, I had given it; with whole-burnt offerings Thou shalt not be pleased.

A sacrifice unto God is a broken spirit; a heart that is broken and humbled God will not despise.

Do good, O Lord, in Thy good pleasure unto Sion, and let the walls of Jerusalem be builded.

Then shalt Thou be pleased with a sacrifice of righteousness, with oblation and whole-burnt offerings.

Then shall they offer bullocks upon Thine altar.

Then we chant the Canon, in Plagal of Fourth Tone:

ODE ONE

Heirmos

Traversing the water as on dry land, * and thereby escaping * from the toils of Egypt's land, * the Israelites cried aloud, proclaiming: * Unto our God and Redeemer let us now sing.

O Saint of God, intercede on our behalf.

To them that entreat thee with contrite hearts * thou grantest true healing * through thy relics now here enshrined; * We cry aloud before them rejoicing: * Unto the martyred King Edward let us now sing.

O Saint of God, intercede on our behalf.

Thy relics were hidden beneath the earth * concealing them safely * from the godless who ruled our land; * but now they are safely entrusted * into the care of the Orthodox Christian Church.

Glory.

Enduring for Christ a martyric death * and thereby acquiring * power and boldness before His throne, * beseech of Him pardon and forgiveness * for those who faithfully honour thy memory.

Both now.

A shelter and refuge art thou for us, * from billows and tempest * of temptations, O most pure one, * wherefore we all fervently entreat thee: * Save us from peril who sail on the sea of life.

ODE THREE

Heirmos

Of the vault of the heavens art Thou, O Lord, Fashioner; * so, too, of the Church art Thou founder; do Thou establish me * in unfeigned love for Thee, * Who art the height of things sought for, * and staff of the faithful, O Thou only Friend of man.

O Saint of God, intercede on our behalf.

As an innocent victim, wast thou slain in thy youth; * by blood-guilty hands wast thou passed a wine-bowl of treachery, * but in death thou showest forth * the wealth of grace thou wast granted * for thy life of service to God and thine earthly realm.

O Saint of God, intercede on our behalf.

As a Martyr and passion-bearing king art thou known, * and throughout the world art thou honoured by all the

Orthodox; * with pure, undoubting faith * the faithful ask thee for healing * for thou workest wonders for those who entreat thine aid.

Glory.

Being pierced through, O Edward, thou wast dragged to thy death; * as a right acceptable victim offered in sacrifice, * thus emulating Christ * Who sacrificed Himself for all * and rose on the third day destroying the bonds of Hades.

Both now.

O immaculate Maiden, thou art a refuge and help * for those in distress and despair, * dragged down by the sea of life; * we call upon thine aid: * guide us in safety to harbour * saving us from peril and harm of the enemy.

We chant the following Troparia in Plagal of Fourth Tone:

Do thou preserve all those who ask thine aid, and venerate thy relics, from all harm and affliction and every calamity O passion-bearing King and Martyr Edward.

In thy good will look thou on me, O all hymned Theotokos; and do thou behold my body's grievous infirmity, and heal thou the cause of my soul's sorrow.

Then the priest commemorates those for whom the Canon is being chanted.

The priest: Have mercy on us, O God, according to Thy great mercy, we pray Thee, hearken and have mercy.

After each petition, we answer: Lord, have mercy. (*thrice*)

Again we pray for pious and Orthodox Christians.

Again we pray for our Bishop [*Name*], and for all our brotherhood in Christ.

Again we pray for mercy, life, peace, health, salvation, visitation, pardon and remission of the sins of the servants of God, all pious and Orthodox Christians who dwell and sojourn in this city, the parishioners and benefactors of this holy temple, and all that serve, chant, labour and gather herein; and for the servants of God [Names], and for the forgiveness of their every transgression, both voluntary and involuntary.

For a merciful and man-befriending God art Thou, and unto Thee do we send up glory, to the Father, and to the Son, and to the Holy Spirit, now and ever, and unto the ages of ages.

The choir: Amen

After these petitions we chant the following Sessional Hymn:

Second Tone

Thou soughtest the heights

Thy relics revealed * in these our times, O martyred Saint * are treasured by us who share the same true faith as thee. * Do thou intercede for us who entreat thee with pure and contrite hearts * for the healing of pains and ills. * O thou who hast boldness before Christ our God.

ODE FOUR

Heirmos

I have hearkened and heard, O Lord, * of Thy dispensation's most awesome mystery; * and I came to knowledge of Thy works, * and I sang the praise of Thy Divinity.

O Saint of God, intercede on our behalf.

Falling down before thee O King, * we extol and bless thee, our comfort in distress; * God hath granted thee the grace to heal * those who praise and honour thee, O Saint of God.

O Saint of God, intercede on our behalf.

Glorifying thee openly, * Christ endued thy relics with grace to heal all ills * that on seeing thy great miracles * we might praise and honour His all holy Name.

Glory.

Celebrating thy memory, * we recall thy wonders and miracles, O Saint, * for thou healest those who seek thine aid * by thy most bold supplications unto Christ.

Both now.

Do thou shine on my darkened soul * with thy light O Virgin and most pure bride of God, * for thou guidest on the path of life * all who seek thine aid, O thou all-lauded one.

ODE FIVE
Heirmos

Lord, enlighten us * by Thy precepts and by Thy commands; * and by the power of Thy lofty arm * bestow Thy peace upon us all, since Thou art Friend of man.

O Saint of God, intercede on our behalf.

Open thou the eyes * of our darkened souls O Saint of God, * as once thy grace-filled relics wondrously * restored the sight of her found worthy to discover them.

O Saint of God, intercede on our behalf.

All who seek thine aid, * praying unto thee O martyred King, * are healed from all disorders of the eyes * and are delivered from affliction of ophthalmia.

Glory.

Though for many years * thou wast hidden deep beneath the earth, * thy sacred relics have now been revealed * and they bestow the gifts of grace on all, O Saint of God.

Both now.

As the Ark of God * thou didst bear the Giver of the Law; * and as the golden and bright candlestick * thou hast without seed given birth to Christ the Source of Light.

ODE SIX
Heirmos

Entreaty do I pour forth unto the Lord, * and to Him do I proclaim all my sorrows, * for many woes fill my heart to repletion, * and lo, my life unto Hades hath now drawn nigh; * like Jonas do I pray to Thee: * Raise me up from corruption, O Lord my God.

O Saint of God, intercede on our behalf.

Entreat thou the God and Saviour of our souls * to deliver us from dangers and perils; * for unto thee * do we flee as our helper, * and we beseech thee come swiftly unto our aid * to save our souls from being lost * in the tempest of life's cruel adversities.

O Saint of God, intercede on our behalf.

God scatt'reth * the bones of man-pleasing men * as the Psalmist David prophesied aforetime; * but God hath shown forth thy relics, O Edward, * as a strong wall and a rampart for those who cry * with fervour and with joy of heart: * Truly wondrous art Thou in thy Saint, O God.

Glory.

Preserve thou * the flock of Christians gathered here * safe from harm caused by heretical doctrine * and strengthen us, * O martyred King Edward, * to remain firm in the Orthodox Christian faith. * And grant thou strength unto our souls * to repel the assaults of the evil one.

Both now.

Thou art known * as the protection of the world * and the temple of the Most High, O Virgin, * thou gavest birth yet remainest a Virgin * and art a fountain of marvellous miracles; * for this cause we cry out to Thee, * from all manner of perils deliver us.

We chant the following Troparia in Plagal of Fourth Tone:

Do thou preserve all those who ask thine aid, and venerate thy relics, from all harm and affliction and every calamity O passion-bearing King and Martyr Edward.

In thy good will, look thou on me, O all hymned Theotokos; and do thou behold my body's grievous infirmity, and heal thou the cause of my soul's sorrow.

Then the priest commemorates as before.

After the petitions, we chant the Kontakion:

Third Tone

Thou didst shine forth in the land of Wessex as a pious king and radiant martyr. For when the enemies of godly order fell upon thee, thou didst bear the wounds and blows and to thy Saviour didst thou speedily depart. But now thou workest a multitude of miracles for them that call upon thee: Rejoice, O holy King and Martyr Edward intercessor for our land.

Then we chant the First Antiphon of the Hymns of Ascent of Fourth Tone:

From my youth do many passions war against me; but do Thou Thyself defend and save me, O my Saviour. (*twice*)

Ye haters of Sion shall be shamed by the Lord; for, like grass, by the fire shall ye be withered. (*twice*)

Glory.

In the Holy Spirit every soul is quickened, and through cleansing is exalted and made radiant by the Triple Unity in a hidden sacred manner.

Both now.

By the Holy Spirit the streams of grace gush forth, watering all creation for the begetting of life.

And straightway we chant the Prokeimenon in Grave Tone:

The righteous man shall be glad in the Lord, and shall hope in Him. (*twice*)

Verse: Hearken, O God, unto my voice when I make supplication unto Thee.

And then we repeat the prokeimenon.

The priest: And that we may be deemed worthy to hear the holy Gospel, let us beseech the Lord our God.

The choir: Lord, have mercy. (*thrice*)

The priest: Wisdom. Upright. Let us hear the holy Gospel. Peace be unto all.

The choir: And to thy spirit.

The priest: The reading is from the holy Gospel according to Saint Luke.

The choir: Glory to Thee, O Lord, glory to Thee.

The priest: Let us attend.

Luke 12:2-7

The Lord said: There is nothing covered, that shall not be revealed; neither hid, that shall not be known. Therefore whatsoever ye have spoken in darkness shall be heard in the light; and that which ye have spoken in the ear in closets shall be proclaimed upon the housetops. And I say unto you my friends, Be not afraid of them that kill the body, and after that have no more that they can do. But I will forewarn you whom ye shall fear: Fear him, which after he hath killed hath power to cast into hell; yea, I say unto you, Fear him. Are not five sparrows sold for two farthings, and not one of them is forgotten before God? But even the very hairs of your head are all numbered. Fear not therefore: ye are of more value than many sparrows.

The choir: Glory to Thee, O Lord, glory to Thee.

Glory. *Second Tone*

By the intercessions of the Martyr Edward, O Merciful One, blot out the multitude of mine offences.

Both now.

By the intercessions of the Theotokos, O Merciful One, blot out the multitude of mine offences.

Verse: Have mercy on me, O God, according to Thy great mercy; and according to the multitude of Thy compassions blot out my transgression.

Plagal of Second Tone
Having laid up all their hope

Enduring a most bitter death, * at the hands of treacherous kinsmen,* an unworthy burial * failed at all to dim thy light, O most blessed Saint. * For thy relics were revealed, * in a wondrous manner,* unto a woman who was blind from birth * who then received her sight * after she discovered thy body * concealed by those who martyred thee * to dishonour thee even after death. * Now as then the power * divine is revealed to us O Saint * as thou dost grant healings unto those * who beseech thine aid with faith.

The priest:

Save O God, Thy people, and bless Thine inheritance; visit Thy world with mercy and compassions; exalt the horn of Orthodox Christians, and send down upon us Thy rich mercies: by the intercessions of our all-immaculate Lady Theotokos and Ever-virgin Mary; by the power of the honoured and life-giving Cross; by the protection of the venerable, heavenly Bodiless Powers; by the supplications of the venerable, glorious Prophet, Forerunner and Baptist John; of the holy, glorious and all-famed Apostles; of our Fathers among the Saints, the great Hierarchs and universal Teachers, Basil the Great, Gregory the Theologian, and John Chrysostom; Athanasius, Cyril, and John the Almsgiver, Patriarchs of Alexandria; Nicholas, Archbishop of Myra, and Spyridon, Bishop of Trimythus, the wonderworkers; of the holy, glorious Great Martyrs, George the Trophy-bearer, Demetrius the Myrrh-streamer, Theodore the Tyro, Theodore the Commander, and Menas the wonder-worker; of the Sacred Martyrs, Haralampus and Eleutherius; of the holy, glorious and triumphantly victorious Martyrs; of our righteous and God-bearing Fathers; of the Holy King of England and Passion-bearer Edward the Martyr; of the holy, righteous Ancestors of God Joachim and Anna; of [*the Saints of the day*] whose memory we keep, and of all Thy Saints: We beseech Thee, Thou only greatly merciful God, hearken unto us sinners who pray unto Thee, and have mercy on us.

The choir: Lord, have mercy. (*twelve times*)

The priest: By the mercy and compassions and love for man of Thine Only-begotten Son, with Whom Thou art blessed, together with Thine All-holy and good and life-creating Spirit, now and ever, and unto the ages of ages.

The choir: Amen.

Then we complete the remaining Odes of the Canon.

ODE SEVEN

Heirmos

Once from out of Judea * did the Children go down to the land of Babylon; * the fire of the furnace * they trampled down while chanting * by their faith in the Trinity: * O God of our Fathers, blessed art Thou.

O Saint of God, intercede on our behalf.

Those who gave thee no honour * were ensnared in the traps that they themselves had set, * whilst those who venerate thee are granted grace and healings * as they cry out most faithfully: * O God of our Fathers, blessed art Thou.

O Saint of God, intercede on our behalf.

Thou didst work a great wonder * when the babe was delivered from deadly malady; * the new-born was named Edward, * in honour of this healing, * as those present cried out with faith: * O God of our Fathers, blessed art Thou.

Glory.

Do thou bless all the founders * of this church dedicated to thee, O martyred Saint; * bless also them that labour * and serve therein O Edward * as they cry out most faithfully: * O God of our Fathers, blessed art Thou.

Both now.

We entreat thee O Virgin * make request to thy Son to grant great mercy unto us. * Deliver from grave error * and from destructive passions * those who cry out most faithfully: * O God of our Fathers, blessed art Thou

ODE EIGHT

Heirmos

The King of Heaven, * Whom all the hosts of Angels hymn * with their chants and praises of glory, * praise ye and exalt Him to the ages for ever.

O Saint of God, intercede on our behalf.

All the assembly * of the true faithful Orthodox * doth rejoice and cry to thee with one voice: * Cleanse us of all stain by thine entreaties, O Martyr.

O Saint of God, intercede on our behalf.

Thy land of England * hath left the straight paths of the Lord * wand'ring on heretical byways; * guide us on the true path of salvation, O Edward.

Glory.

We entreat thee, * do thou intercede for all * of the Christians of this land, O King Edward, * that the true and genuine Church therein may prosper.

Both now.

Rescue O Lady * my poor and truly wretched soul * from the snares and traps of the demons; * free me from the bonds of sin and lead me to salvation.

ODE NINE

Heirmos

Most rightly we confess thee * as our God's Birthgiver, * we who through thee have been saved, O thou Virgin most pure; * with choirs of bodiless Angels, thee do we magnify.

O Saint of God, intercede on our behalf.

O Edward we beseech thee * as a king and Martyr * who hast much boldness with God to entreat Him for us, * that we be granted forgiveness, * since He is merciful.

O Saint of God, intercede on our behalf.

Thy relics pour forth healings * of the soul and body * for those who venerate them with compunction, O Saint, * and do thou succour, O Edward, * all those who flee to thee.

Glory.

Make fervent supplication, * in thy tender mercy, * for those who venerate thee through thine icon, O Saint, * that Christ our God and our Saviour * grant us full healthfulness.

Both now.

In thee O Theotokos, * we have a true weapon * against the demon's assaults and their envy O Maid; wherefore we honour thee rightly * calling upon thine aid.

It is truly meet to call the blest, the Theotokos, the ever-blessed and all-immaculate and Mother of our God. More honourable than the Cherubim, and beyond compare more glorious than the Seraphim, thee who without corruption gavest birth to God the Word, the very Theotokos, thee do we magnify.

Then the priest censes the Holy Table and the people, or the house where the Canon is being chanted; and we chant the following Megalynaria:

Anointed with holy chrism by Christ our God, * O crowned Passion-bearer, * thou didst meekly submit to death, * thereby gaining laurels * of glory and wonderworking, * O champion of monastics, King and Martyr Edward.

As a faithful servant of the Lord, * armed with prayer and labour, * thou didst rule with true piety * as a noble monarch * and passion-bearing Martyr; * O Edward we beseech thee shelter us by thy prayers.

Though thy sacred relics were concealed * in the earth and hidden * from men's sight, O most honoured King, * yet they were revealed in * these latter days, O Edward, * bestowing cures and healings on those who flee to thee.

Thy most holy relics are like a spring, * washing all who kiss them * with outpouring of grace divine, * cleansing from defilement * and filling all with fragrance; * O Edward we acclaim and honour thy memory.

O all ye arrays of Angelic hosts * with the holy Baptist * the Apostles' twelve-numbered band, * all the Saints together as well as God's Birthgiver, * pray make ye intercession for our deliverance.

The reader: Holy God, Holy Mighty, Holy Immortal, have mercy on us. (*thrice*)

Glory to the Father, and to the Son, and to the Holy Spirit; both now and ever, and unto the ages of ages. Amen.

All-holy Trinity, have mercy on us. Lord, be gracious unto our sins. Master, pardon our iniquities. Holy One, visit and heal our infirmities for Thy Name's sake.

Lord, have mercy. (*thrice*)

Glory to the Father, and to the Son, and to the Holy Spirit, both now and ever, and unto the ages of ages. Amen.

Our Father, Which art in the heavens, hallowed be Thy Name. Thy kingdom come. Thy will be done, on earth as it is in Heaven. Give us this day our daily bread. And forgive us our debts, as we forgive our debtors. And lead us not into temptation, but deliver us from the evil one.

The priest: For Thine is the kingdom, and the power, and the glory, of the Father, and of the Son, and of the Holy Spirit, now and ever, and unto the ages of ages.

The reader: Amen. Lord, have mercy. (*twelve times)*

Then we chant the following Troparia:

Fourth Tone

Celebrating the newly manifest commemoration of the holy King Edward who shone forth of old in the virtues and suffered undeservedly, and bowing down before his precious relics in gladness we cry out: Wondrous art Thou in Thy Saint, O God!

Plagal of Second Tone

Have mercy on us, Lord, have mercy on us; for lacking as we are in all defence, this supplication do we sinners offer unto Thee, as our Master: Have mercy on us.

Glory.

L ord, have mercy on us, for in Thee have we placed all our trust; be not wroth with us greatly, nor do Thou remember our iniquities; but look upon us even now, since Thou art compassionate, and do Thou redeem us from our enemies; for Thou art our God, and we Thy people; all are the works of Thy hands, and upon Thy name have we called.

Both now.

D o thou open the portal of compassion unto us, O most blessed Theotokos; for hoping in thee, let us not fail, we pray; through thee may we be delivered from adversities, for thou art the salvation of the Christian race.

And the priest, having commemorated again the faithful for whom the Canon is being chanted, makes the dismissal.

The priest: Wisdom.

The reader: Holy Father, bless.

The priest: Blessed is He that is, even Christ our God, always, now and ever and unto the ages of ages.

The reader: Amen. The Lord God make steadfast the holy and blameless faith of the pious and Orthodox Christians, with His holy Church and this city [*or* monastery, *or* town *or* countryside *or* island] unto the ages of ages. Amen.

The priest: Most holy Theotokos, save us.

The reader: More honourable than the Cherubim, and beyond compare more glorious than the Seraphim, thee who without corruption gavest birth to God the Word, the very Theotokos, thee do we magnify.

The priest: Glory to Thee, O God, our hope, glory to Thee.

The reader: Glory to the Father, and to the Son, and to the Holy Spirit; both now and ever, and unto the ages of ages. Amen. Lord, have mercy (*thrice*). Holy Father, bless.

The priest: May Christ our true God, through the intercessions of His all-immaculate Mother; of the holy right-believing King of England and Passion-bearer Edward the Martyr; of the holy and righteous ancestors of God, Joachim and Anna, and of all the Saints: have mercy on us, and save us, for He is good and the Friend of Man.

The choir: Amen.

After this, as the faithful kiss the icon of Saint Edward, the following Troparia are chanted with prostrations:

Second Tone

When he took Thee

Hearken unto those who now fall down * at the shrine of thy sacred relics and with great fervour extol * all thy wondrous miracles, O right-believing King, * and attend unto our requests, * bestowing deliv'rance, * saving us from perils and all manner of distress; * since thou hast boldness before Christ, * beseech him always to have mercy * on those, O Edward, who with faith honour thee.

Plagal of Fourth Tone

LADY, do thou receive the supplications of thy slaves, and deliver us from every affliction and necessity.

Second Tone

UNTO thee do I commit mine every hope, O Mother of God; guard me under thy shelter.

The priest: Through the prayers of our holy Fathers, Lord Jesus Christ, our God, have mercy on us.

The choir: Amen.